YOUR TIME, YOUR WAY

Time Well Managed, Life Well Lived

By Carl Pullein

ROTHSTEIN
PUBLISHING
A Division of Rothstein Associates Inc.
www.rothsteinpublishing.com

Print – ISBN: 978-1-944480-08-13 (Softcover)
Print – ISBN: 978-1-944480-08-06 (Hardcover)
EPUB – 978-1-944480-08-37
WEB PDF – 978-1-944480-08-20
AUDIO BOOK – 978-1-944480-08-44

Library of Congress Control Number (LCCN): 2024930919

ROTHSTEIN
PUBLISHING
A Division of Rothstein Associates Inc.
4 Arapaho Road
Brookfield, Connecticut 06804 USA
203.740.7400
info@rothstein.com
www.rothsteinpublishing.com

WHAT PEOPLE LIKE YOU ARE SAYING ABOUT *YOUR TIME, YOUR WAY*

"Life can often become overwhelming with the multitude of issues demanding immediate attention. This can lead to missed deadlines and, most importantly, compromised family time as I scramble to catch up with work. TSS has been a game-changer for me, helping me remain focused on what truly matters in both my home and work life. TSS has truly made a positive impact on my productivity and overall well-being. I wholeheartedly recommend it to anyone seeking a comprehensive approach to managing their time and achieving a healthy work-life balance." – **Jeff Jackson**

"It's been challenging to focus on what's important when much of my time is committed to 40+ hours/week at work and the routines of maintaining a house, domestic chores, and time with my spouse. When I blocked out time on my dream calendar for my areas of focus and desired core work and compared it to my actual calendar including my regular job and routines, it was an eye opener.

I am successfully using the Time Sector System at work. I complete my daily planning every day and weekly plan at the end of the work week. I appreciate the simplicity of the Time Sector System. Planning for the upcoming week IS all that you need to focus on." – **Jana Palermo**

"I am not a high-powered executive climbing the corporate ladder. I am a full-time working mom and I manage the care for my mother, who is in an assisted living facility. For the last couple of years, things have gotten more complicated. The stress kept building and I became overwhelmed. When I started missing appointments and deadlines, I realized that I had to act.

I tried the GTD system, but it wasn't sustainable for me. I was spending a lot of time organizing. After all that organization, I often couldn't find the information I needed.

Your idea of organizing by time was brilliantly simple. That's what I need, a simple system that *works*. I've only been using the time sector system for a few weeks, but I am already noticing the benefits. It is funny how a system can change the way you think. By putting tasks into buckets based on when I need to get them done, I am significantly better at prioritizing." – Ann Ramey, Hawaii

"Your vision of the Time Sector System has been helping me for 3 years. My aim is not necessarily to be more productive, but above all to be better organized so as to do things better. The results are there. I'm more efficient and less stressed!" – Guigueek

"I have multiple projects, clients, and tasks … at any one time. Working fully from home, motivation is a big issue, and I found it easy to get distracted and drift off course. I'd spent 18 months(!) trying different productivity tools to no avail – time blocking, to-do lists, daily planning, Trello, etc. – and without a coherent system or process, they didn't work for me.

The Time Sector System… changed my relationship with time. I'd previously put tasks into 'buckets' by project or by client, rather than when they needed to be done, which made managing my diary across all my workstreams confusing and rather disorganized. Moving to a system with 'this week,' 'coming up,' and 'future' – planning for *when* things need to be done, regardless of *what* they are – has helped me to be more focused, to plan my diary better, and feel more in control. I can't imagine working without the system and will be using it for a long time to come!" – Tracey Warren BSc (Hons) FMAAT

"'It doesn't matter how long your to-do list is, if you don't have enough time to do the tasks.' This quote truly resonated with me. I often found myself feeling totally overwhelmed and defeated by my endless to-do lists. The Time Sector System taught me a very effective method to simplify what is important *now* and how to stay focused on those critical tasks without feeling overwhelmed or depressed with other tasks that must wait. The method reduces distraction and overwhelm. It's a unique approach that is simply brilliant.

The Time Sector System is a life raft that taught me to efficiently navigate through my tasks. I've been using the system for 6 months, and it truly is a lifesaver. The simplicity of this system can work for anyone!" – **Michelle Philips**

"The Time Sector System has been the pivotal ingredient for my success in all areas of my life. TSS can't be mentioned without a few of your other teachings: COD, 2+8 prioritization (I do 3+7 but the principal is the same), as well as daily and weekly reviews. TSS is the culmination of all these systems that have allowed me to pay off debt, get married, go on multiple vacations, adopt my wife's daughter, do countless home renovations, and build an office addition, all while running a transportation business with 30 employees. TSS helped me when COVID shut down my business for 9 months, it has helped my business become debt-free, and it has helped me grow revenues by 40% in 5 years.

A lot of work was required on my part, but TSS helped me stay focused and on task. Before TSS I never knew what success for that day looked like. I was always feeling that I was missing something, even if I knew I had added it to my task manager. TSS has allowed me to say "these tasks are important This Week" without actually making up an artificial date. TSS has allowed me to sleep easier at night knowing that what is important for This Week is readily available and only a click away: grab a few tasks after looking at my calendar and know what success for that day looks like." – **Brian Walsh**

DEDICATION

For my wife and little Louis, without either of them,
this book would not exist.

ACKNOWLEDGMENTS

There are so many people who have, over the years, helped me to bring this book to you. There are too many to mention individually, but you know who you are, so thank you.

I must thank my former General Manager at Carnell Motor Group, Andrew Donovan, who inspired me to pursue my passion for time management, productivity, and personal organization. Then there are the students I have taught here in Korea who showed me a different way to approach work – some good, some bad.

In addition, I would like to thank Ernie Hayden, who introduced me to Phil Rothstein, my publisher, who got the ball rolling to bring this book to print, and to all my coaching clients who, over the years, have challenged me in so many wonderful ways to find solutions to seemingly impossible challenges. We did it! We found those solutions.

And finally, but by no means least, thank you to my wife for allowing me to pursue this journey and listening to my time management ramblings on so many car journeys across Korea. And little Louis, our beloved Yorkie, whose demands for long walks by the beach enabled me to have the time to step back and think things through and produce the content I produce each week.

CONTENTS

FOREWORD BY
ED WHITMORE

I am a busy screenwriter forever trying to keep the encroaching fire of multiple deadlines at bay. About three years ago that fire wasn't so much encroaching as burning down the house and I knew something had to give. I was lurching from one missed deadline to another and locked in a cycle of working seven-day weeks, grudgingly foregoing family time and generally feeling one step behind, sometimes ten steps.

My stressful predicament ultimately sent me on a deep dive into the burgeoning world of productivity and time management media. Nothing really stuck until I stumbled on one of Carl Pullein's winningly clear and actionable videos on how to get the most out of ToDoist, which swiftly led me to his range of online courses.

It is not an understatement to say that enrolling in Carl's brilliant *Time Sector System* course proved to be a life-changing decision. But that change did not happen overnight. Two of the attributes that mark Carl out from an ocean of over-promising, under-delivering productivity gurus are his honesty and realism – he doesn't pretend there are quick fixes or that the road from disorganized to organized is short and hurdle-free.

Instead, Carl encourages you to build a productivity system that follows certain core principles and structures but that – ultimately, crucially – can be fine-tuned to meet your own specific needs.

Once I'd got to grips with the Time Sector System, I felt liberated and focused like never before. Just by sticking to a few good habits — capturing every new task rather than deluding myself, and taking five minutes to plan the following day, to name but two – I suddenly felt ahead of the game and not behind! Instead of being burdened by a mile-long to-do list I had a system that kept me focused on my major projects, while miraculously allowing time for the myriad smaller tasks and unforeseen things that "just come up."

"If it ain't broke, don't fix it," as the saying goes, and three years on, while I occasionally tweak a label here, a task heading there, my use of Carl's system remains remarkably unchanged. And, tellingly, I have not been tempted to suspend or even pause its daily implementation.

The reason for this goes to the heart of Carl's productivity ethos. Basically it's incredibly user-friendly and easy to maintain, qualities that derive from the underlying principle that the system should work for you, not the other way around. So many productivity systems are unrealistically complicated, time-consuming, and ultimately unsustainable. In contrast, Carl offers an approach that is lean, flexible, intuitive, and fleet-footed, reflecting a refreshingly simple premise: when all's said and done, only two questions truly matter: what is the task, and when are you going to do it?

As a TV scriptwriter and executive producer I often used to find myself caught on the horns of a dilemma – namely, my days were filled with essential meetings and calls but if I didn't put in serious writing time I'd be shortchanging the most important part of my job. The proverbial circle that couldn't be squared. The only solution seemed to be burning the midnight oil or, more often than not, the 4 a.m. oil...

No longer. In *Your Time, Your Way* Carl delivers both the tools and the methodology to truly take charge of your diary, your time and, ultimately, your life. Speaking personally, implementing these ideas and strategies has been a game-changer for me. Liberated by a system that optimizes the time/work balance so effectively, I now always know where I'm supposed to be and what I'm supposed to be doing. And the concomitant savings in terms of time and energy have been as astonishing as they are welcome. Now, rather than merely hoping to spend more time with my family or taking exercise, those aspirations have become firm and regular fixtures.

Your Time, Your Way is a brilliantly comprehensive, all-in-one-place summation of Carl's productivity ethos that's practical, inspiring, and definitive. But its scope extends far beyond the workplace to encompass our life goals, spiritual needs, general happiness, and wellbeing. With his infectious blend of enthusiasm and pragmatism, Carl outlines clear, actionable steps that will turn seemingly unreachable ambitions into concrete realities. He urges us to think deeply about what's truly important to us and to focus and prioritize our precious time accordingly. As such, **Your Time, Your Way** transcends being just another time management book – it is nothing less than a guide to living your best life: happy, balanced, ordered, and – of course – productive.

Ed Whitmore

May, 2024

Introduction

My time management and productivity obsession began nearly thirty years ago. I vividly remember painstakingly drawing out exam revision timetables with a pencil and ruler when my middle and high school exams approached. I would use different colored pens for each subject and create beautiful timetables with built-in break periods and days off.

I loved it! I was great at creating the timetable; just terrible at doing revision and exams.

My love of productivity and time management comes from competitive athletics. As a teenager, I was encouraged to run by an inspiring teacher, Mr. Farrow. He encouraged me to take up cross-country running, and this was the first time I found myself good at anything. I was not a model pupil and languished in the bottom sets in all the key subjects: mathematics, English, and science. But when I took up cross-country running, I found myself at the head of the pack. It seemed I was a natural!

My coaches gave me training programs, and all I had to do was to follow the schedule. Those schedules taught me how to manage my time. I went to school, and then after school, I ran. Sometimes at the running club, other times on my own. Then I came home and did my homework. I quickly learned that the key to success at running (and academic studies) was consistently following a plan and applying a little persistence.

The training schedules and the routines I learned about as a teenage athlete became revision timetables and schedules in my schoolwork. This resulted in my grades rising. I never quite made it to the "A" sets, but I no longer languished in the bottom "D" sets.

All the pieces were falling into place. I was learning about structure, routine, persistence, and, most importantly, knowing what I wanted.

Not long after joining the workforce when I began my first day as a new car sales executive, I was introduced to my sales manager, David Cox. As I was ushered into David's office, I noticed an open A5 desk diary in the center of his desk that showed an entire week across two pages. To complement this diary, a pile of papers was neatly fanned out in perfect alignment on the right-hand side of David's desk.

It struck me that this was an organized person. Yet, I had no evidence of this except for how clean and organized David's desk was. Everything seemed organized around his A5 diary; it was the centerpiece of his desk.

Thirty years later, I spoke with David about this, and he mentioned that his diary is still his number one organization tool. He now uses a digital calendar, but the way he uses it is the same way he used that A5 desk diary all those years ago.

If you think about it and want to know where you need to be, when, and with whom, your calendar is the perfect tool.

You may have heard of something called the *Bullet Journal*. The Bullet Journal is a paper-based system where you take a plain notebook and design your own way of managing your tasks and appointments. The centerpiece of the journal is – you guessed it – your diary, which you draw out yourself. You can create boxes, lines, or any way to show your daily appointments and commitments. If you are artistic and want to practice your artistic skills, the Bullet Journal is a beautiful way to do it!

David's boss, our general manager, was Andrew Donovan. When I was introduced to Andrew, in his office was… wait for it… a gorgeous A4 black leather diary taking center stage on his desk and a perfectly lined set of papers on the right-hand side. Andrew also had an expensive-looking blue Waterman ball pen neatly placed on the open desk diary. (He was the big boss, after all).

It was an almost perfect copy of what I had seen on David's desk earlier, save for being larger and a little more expensive in appearance.

What was it about these two gentlemen that gave the impression they were organized and on top of their work? Part of what led me to believe that was the cleanliness of their desks. It was a first impression, but seeing their open diaries with their appointments neatly written in gave me a sense of focused organization.

While you may not use a paper-based planner today, the principles used back then are the same principles today. If you want to be on top of your work and know how much time you have, you'd better ensure your stuff is organized.

Over the months, the more I learned about Andrew's working style, the more inspired I became. Andrew was the most organized person I had met. Whenever Andrew held a management meeting, he would carry a spiral reporter's notebook; when he asked someone to do something, he would write it down in that notebook. You knew Andrew would never forget to follow up with you, and his management team always succeeded in getting things done.

The experience of working with Andrew and David set me on a course of having a well-organized diary. Andrew's impeccable yet simple time management system inspired others. It inspired David, and it certainly inspired me.

I remember discovering where Andrew bought his desk diary and traveling over the Pennines in the north of England (around a two-hour drive) to purchase one. Looking back today, I see it was one of the best purchases I ever made because it began my journey of using tools to manage my life.

Before buying that diary, I, like most people, tried to remember everything in my head. It's the worst time management system ever invented! As David Allen, author *of Getting Things Done*, says, "Your head is a crappy office." You may have noticed that your brain does not understand time; it only knows something has to be done and will remind you about it at the worst possible time. For example, I'm sure you've been reminded to turn off a light or lock your back door when in your car halfway between work and home. It never reminds you as you leave your home.

I've gone through all sorts of different time management and organization systems, from my first Filofax in the late eighties to the Franklin Planner in the early nineties and finally going all in on digital planning when I got my first iPhone in 2009.

The basic principles of time management haven't changed. Benjamin Franklin, one of the Founding Fathers, kept a simple diary/journal listing how he would organize his day. There was time for dining, resting, reading/self-education, sleeping, and work. Throughout history, the most creative and productive people have succeeded because they took control of their time. They knew what they wanted and carved out time each day to create. It didn't happen by accident.

Over the last twenty years, there appears to have been a shift away from this wisdom of first establishing what is important to you and building your days and weeks on that foundation. Today, it's all about managing projects, tasks, and appointments. What we value and want to spend time on has sunk to the bottom of the task-list pit.

What teachers like Hyrum Smith, Stephen Covey, Jim Rohn, and Earl Nightingale taught us has mostly been replaced by app developers who want to sell you the latest, shiniest tool to get you hooked on organizing and moving stuff around.

Instead of establishing your governing values and the principles of first-things-first (i.e. you, your family, your dreams, your aspirations), you are seduced into tools that stop you from thinking about what you want and instead focus you on task completion. That doesn't get meaningful work done! That causes the very thing you are trying to avoid – overwhelm, stress, anxiety, and, ultimately, breakdown.

I began to think, what kind of time management system would work in a world with ever-increasing input from email and message services such as What's App, Teams, and Slack, where deadlines were no longer months but often weeks or days away? There had to be a better way!

This led to the development of the principles around the **COD** productivity system. COD stands for **C**ollect, **O**rganize, and **D**o, and every sound productivity system has this at its core; it's nothing new. You need to *collect* all the inputs you receive in a trusted place – a digital inbox in your notes app, a task manager, or a simple notebook. No matter what tool you use to collect all these commitments, events, and ideas, you need to trust that you will collect everything there.

Then you set aside some time to *organize* everything you collected. Where will you put it so you will not forget it? For that, we have task managers, notes apps, and calendars.

And finally, you need to be *doing the work*. Nothing else matters if you have an excellent collection system and everything is beautifully organized, but you aren't doing the work, you are procrastinating. All systems require you to be doing the work.

Many pour scorn on the prioritization method of older time management systems. The argument is that no matter how essential you decide something is, if you don't have the tool or are in the right place or with the right person, no amount of urgency will help you to complete that task unless you pick up the right tool, move to the right place or person. And that is perfectly true.

However, we live in the twenty-first century, and most of these productivity systems were developed in the 1980s and 1990s. Technology has moved on a lot since then. In 1997, you had to be in your workplace with your work computer to reply to your work email. Very few companies provided their employees with laptops, and the dawn of the smartphone, as we know it today, was a decade away. We also worked mainly with paper files and large filing cabinets. It was a different world thirty years ago!

Today, your smartphone has more power than even the most powerful office computer from the mid-1990s. You can respond to your emails, write reports, and update spreadsheets. You can even design a presentation, all from that little device in your pocket.

Communications are very different today, too. With Microsoft Teams, FaceTime and Zoom, we no longer need to be face-to-face with people to have a meaningful meeting. And these communications can be done from almost anywhere using any digital device.

Knowing what to work on and when is possibly the most challenging areas of our lives. There are many distractions, from the traditional distractions of our colleagues, customers, and bosses' demands, to notifications from Facebook, LinkedIn, Instagram and X, all demanding immediate attention. The boundary between our work and personal lives is blurred, and it is almost impossible to hide away and get on with some deep, meaningful, focused work.

To counter this, I realized that *prioritization* was the key. Enough inputs are coming at you daily to fill up a whole month of work. It would be impossible to manage all that work if you do not start to prioritize what you need to do.

Once you know what is important, the only thing you need to know is *when* a task needs doing. If a task does not need to be done this week, don't worry about it. All you need to know when you plan your week is what needs to be done this week to have a successful week. And this is where the *Time Sector System* comes in.

The Time Sector System manages your tasks by *when they need to be done.*

Over the last few years, these systems have transformed my productivity and thousands of others through my blog, YouTube channel, podcast, and online courses. They have brought some sense, calm, and deliberate intention back into people's lives by providing a system, or process, for doing work. It's based on what matters most to you instead of putting out fires. It's less about organizing and shuffling stuff around and more about identifying what matters to you through learning what *your* areas of focus are *and ensuring these are front and center of your day.*

It means when you start a new day, you are clear about what needs to be accomplished, and you know that what you plan to do that day is meaningful and moves important things forward. It puts a stop to that feeling that all you are doing is waiting to be told what to do next and trying to keep a long line of plates spinning. In other words, *it puts you back in control of your life.*

This book is divided into a number of sections. First, we will discover what is important to you with your eight areas of focus.

Once you have established your areas of focus, we will then move on to learning about COD and the Time Sector System.

After that, we will look at the common issues people face, and I will show you ways to eliminate these issues through building processes.

From there, you will gain strategies to be able to build your own system, a system that works for you, so you can begin to focus on the things that are most important to you.

To get the most out of this book, I would recommend you take your time. Do the exercises. These exercises are designed to assist you in building your own system. There may be suggestions and ideas that don't fit how you work or how you run your life. That's fine; it does not mean the system as a whole won't work for you. I remember when I first wrote about managing projects in a notes app, and some readers immediately responded by saying it would not work for them. They never gave it a chance.

Any change in the way we do things will feel uncomfortable at first. But nothing will change unless you try something new. When I began managing projects in my notes app, it felt strange for a few weeks. I often found myself being pulled back to trying to manage projects in my task manager, yet I persisted, and now it's just a natural way.

As you read through this book, keep an open mind. The ideas and methods work. They've already worked for thousands of people and transformed their relationship with time. If you are ready to clear your backlogs, work on the things that matter to you, and get back in control of your day, then read on!

"Lack of time is not the problem. Lack of direction is the problem." – Zig Ziglar

Carl Pullein

Gangneung, South Korea

May, 2024

1

Task Centered Time Management Does Not Work

Do you feel that no matter how much you do each day, more stuff is added to your to-do list than you completed? It wasn't long ago we were promised that digital technology would enable us to get more work done in less time. Well, it might have helped us to get more work done, but a side effect of that has been an exponential increase in the amount of work that comes our way.

Twenty-years ago, most people were struggling to cope with the number of emails they were getting, that number hasn't reduced; it's increased at a frightening rate. Then along came Slack and Microsoft Teams, and now not only do you need to stay on top of email, but you also need to be responding to hundreds of internal messages each day.

In addition to the increase in these forms of communication, you are still expected to get your work done. You're still expected to write proposals for your customers, deal with client requests and work on the numerous projects your boss has given to you.

And if that isn't enough, you still have to attend meetings and training sessions. And that's before you begin to look at what you want to do in your personal life.

How does anyone keep their head above water when all this is coming at you day after day?

Fortunately, there are a number of ways to regain control of your day. It won't be easy, but it is simple to learn.

I've learned over the years I've been obsessed with time management and productivity that the more complex a system is, the less likely you will stick with it. Many good systems have come and gone over the years but owing to their complexity, they have fallen by the wayside.

Your Time, Your Way is not going to give you a system that will be out of date almost the moment you read it. Your Time, Your Way will give you a framework on which you can build. Given that you will be learning a framework, advances in technology will not break your system, if anything, advances will enhance your system.

Before you dive deep into this book, I want to share some strategies that will help you get the most out of it and, more importantly, help you create a time management and productivity system that works for *you*.

I understand the temptation to get straight to setting up the system. That's fine, but in many ways, if you start there, it will be like putting a sticking plaster on a gaping wound. It will be a temporary fix to a problem that has deeper roots.

Our time management issues are caused by trying to fit in more than we have time for. This is particularly easy when at work. Traditionally, we work for a set number of hours in the day, and unless you are a shift worker, you will likely do that work during the day. A typical workday is, at least in theory, eight to nine hours, and while today these times are blurred, this is where most of our problems start.

We tend to underestimate how long a task will take. We think an email reply will take two minutes or less, and ten minutes later, we hit send. What happened? Well, you were likely interrupted by a colleague, or your phone beeped. Or initially, what seemed an easy reply was a little more complicated than you thought. These little disruptions and miscalculations happen throughout the day, and at the end of your workday, you feel there's still so much to do, and you'll be correct. There will *always* be a lot to do.

This approach to work is task-focused or, if you like something a little more scientific, production-focused. Yet, it's often unfocused production. It's production for *the sake of production* – although I am sure it doesn't feel that way. What are you completing? Does it matter? If you look carefully at what you are completing, you are likely prioritizing the urgent over the important. Urgent tasks generally come from other people; they are the most difficult to ignore.

Look back at what you did yesterday. How much of what you did moved an important project or goal forward? How much was reacting to events? Answering questions from colleagues or customers, rectifying mistakes previously made, or the monotonous low-value box-ticking tasks? If you're like most people, you will have spent over 90% of your time yesterday doing stuff that didn't matter in the long term.

Part of this issue is we have become task focused – looking at how much we have to do, instead of being time focused – looking at how much time we have available.

Prior to the digital revolution (when many people began using digital calendars, notes apps, and task managers), we used desk diaries. These were great because there was a natural limitation – the size of your diary. If you inhabited a corner office, you likely had an A4-sized leather-bound diary. If you were anyone else, you probably had an A5 faux-leather one, often handed to you by your company.

There were many designs for these diaries, but the most common was a two-page week to view. Each day had its own column, and two-thirds of the column was dedicated to your calendar for the day. Here, you would schedule your meetings and appointments and block out time for focused work. The bottom third of the column was six to eight lines for notes that most people used as their to-do list.

This meant you were restricted to less than eight to-dos each day. This was a manageable number of tasks.

These desk diaries were great because, at a glance, you could instantly see if you had overbooked yourself. It was there, staring at you in the face! It was as if a voice was screaming at you to reschedule appointments or cancel meetings. You would *never* consider adding two meetings or commitments at the same time. You could instantly see you had a conflict.

In the digital world, we don't have that. We can add hundreds of tasks to a task manager, which will eat them up without complaint. Unfortunately, you don't get to see what you have added unless you go in and look for it. And with every other kind of distraction competing for your attention, you won't look.

And digital calendars are worse! You now get digital invites to meetings with the option to accept, maybe, or decline with the click of a button. So you click – after all, who has time to check their calendar, me? Later, you discover you've double-booked yourself. For the most part, this is all hidden away behind your screen. Few of us have our calendars open on our desktops. At some point, you'll have to sort this out, another set of tasks you must do.

Task-centered productivity doesn't work! The problem with today's thinking on time management – and, by extension, productivity – it's now all about checking tasks off a list and trying to juggle more meetings than there are hours in the day.

It wasn't always like that. In the late 80s and early 90s, Stephen Covey and Hyrum Smith identified the same problems; we had moved away from focusing our time and attention on being better and instead had become unhappy, stressed-out, box-ticking automatons.

Something has changed over the last twenty years or so. In the 90s, many individuals and companies recognized the need for balance and development of the individual. The focus was on what mattered, not how much could be done in the minimum time. Many employees were sent on time management courses, and they did help. Likely, those colleagues you work with who began their careers in the 1990s are less stressed and more organized than their younger counterparts. Today, we've swung back to being focused on doing more and more and lost sight of what matters.

You can see the results of this change. More people than ever are suffering from mental health issues. Vast numbers of people are off sick with stress-related illnesses, and customer service across whole swaths of industries has been reduced to an anonymous chatbot (or, if you're lucky, a ticket number).

When it comes to time management, you are not managing *time*. Time is fixed, and it resets every day. It's an incredible gift that will keep giving until the day you die. If you wasted the twenty-four hours you got yesterday, you won't get that back. Instead, you get a new twenty-four hours today.

What you are managing is your *activities*. When you begin a new day, you are free to do what you like with the hours you have that day. You could, if you choose to do so, call in sick and stay in bed all day. Alternatively, you could get up, jump into your exercise clothes, and do an hour's exercise. That's the great thing about time! Each day, you are free to choose what you do with it. It's *your* time, and you can use it *your* way.

Many people I have worked with over the years complain they are busy. They are too busy to exercise, too busy to take their daughter to the park, too busy to get enough sleep, and too busy to start the business they've always dreamed of starting. If that resonates with you, ask yourself: *What are you busy doing? Probably not what is important to you.*

If you take the time to establish your areas of focus, (What is important to you) when you move on to the chapters that give you the system and strategies to manage your day with clarity and focus, I can assure you, you will no longer get to the end of the day feeling like you've done nothing all day but run around doing busy work.

The *Time Sector System*—a simple way to manage your to-dos based on when you will do them--will help you to get on top of your work. It will prevent backlogs from building up and give you clarity on what needs to be done each week. However, if you don't know what is important to you, all you will be doing is managing busy-work more efficiently. You will still feel unfulfilled at the end of each day and feel empty inside. That's not what this book is about. This book is here to help you get clear on what is important to you, no matter where you are in life, so that when you finish each day, you feel fulfilled and excited to begin your *next* twenty-four hours.

What the **Time Sector System** will *not* give you is more shiny tools to play with. The Time Sector System is a system designed to ensure you are doing what matters so you have more time to do the things you want to do. It will work with almost any time management and productivity tools you are using today, and it will grow with you as you grow.

It's important to understand that reading this book and doing nothing will not change anything. To get the most out of this book, do the exercises and take your time. This is not a quick fix. You will need to step back, think, organize, and build processes. The effort, though, will be rewarding. You will learn to develop your way of managing your activities. You will find time to do the things you've always felt you didn't have time for, and your work tasks will no longer be building up because you will already have eliminated the low-value stuff that can be ignored.

That may sound like a dream today, but a little time and reading through this book will give you the skills and know-how to finally take control of your time in your way. Enjoy the journey.

Let's get started!

2

Laying The Foundations

"You can't build a great building on a weak foundation. You must have a solid foundation if you're going to have a strong superstructure." – Gordon B. Hinckley

All great systems are built on solid foundations. Similarly, before you can start to build a solid time management system, you first need to build your foundations. Without a strong base, you will find that while the Time Sector System will tell you what needs to be done (a good thing), there will be no structure or level of prioritization (a bad thing), and you will be swamped by the amount you feel you need to do (a really bad thing).

In this book, you will be shortly given a new tool to manage your tasks and projects. However, just telling you to gather together all your tasks and projects and put them into the Time Sector System will not solve the underlying problems you are likely to face with your time management and productivity. Without developing a strong base – a foundation, if you like – all you will be doing is churning out tasks all day with no purpose or direction. It will be like spending all day putting out fires. That's a recipe for stress and illness.

You first need to discover what is important to you. Yes, for a brief time, you are going to need to be selfish!

Your Foundations are the Things in Your Life That are Important to You

What is important to you? What really matters today? Without first establishing what's important to you, you will discover you are working on what's important to *others*. While that may appear benevolent, it ultimately leads to you working on everyone else's work and not your own work, leaving you unfulfilled. (But everyone else is happy because they got their projects done).

When you don't know what's important to you, you will find your task list filling up with unimportant tasks that keep you busy but achieve very little. You want to change that so that what you do daily is focused on your priorities, desires and plans for the future and the work you are employed to do.

In this first section, you will learn how to lay the foundations of your system. You will discover what is important to you and what the eight areas of focus mean to you and establish what you can do each day or week to keep them balanced and healthy.

This part of the system ensures you do what matters to you and prevents you from being caught up in a cycle of overwhelm and stress.

So, let us begin with the ultimate foundation: your areas of focus.

3

The Eight Areas of Life We All Have In Common

"The most important things in life aren't things."
– Anthony J. D'Angelo

In time management and productivity systems, there are three basic parts. At the simplest level are *tasks*. Things that need to be done to move something forward or to maintain equilibrium. Then there are *projects* and *processes*. Projects and processes are similar in that they are groups of related tasks designed to reach a clearly defined outcome by a specified date. Finally, areas of *focus* are things you have identified as important to you that you want to maintain and improve. These relate to your finances, health, career, and other essential areas of your life.

Areas of focus are the higher-level parts of your life that are important to you and, when maintained in a way that satisfies how you define them, help you keep your life in balance. Suppose you identify health (an area of focus) as an important part of your life; a regularly recurring task telling you to exercise will appear in your daily task list (or you have it as an event on your calendar). Aside from ensuring you exercise as frequently as you decide you want, you have it in balance. If, for whatever reason, you stop exercising, you will soon find yourself feeling as if something is missing – there will be a sense of guilt because you are no longer exercising.

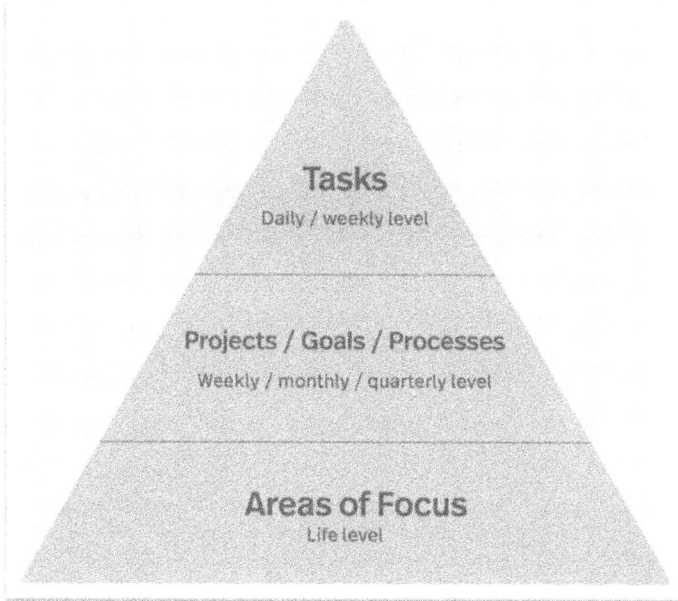

There are eight areas in total. We all share these areas as they are fundamental to a functioning person, no matter where you are. If you neglect any of these areas of your life, you will feel something is wrong—like a nagging voice in your head telling you something.

Let's look at the eight areas of focus:

- Family and relationships
- Career/business
- Finances
- Health and Fitness
- Spirituality
- Lifestyle and life experiences
- Personal Development
- Purpose in life

While we share all eight of these, the difference between us is how we define what each means and the order of priority in which we put them.

How you prioritize these depends on where you are in life right now. For instance, if you are in your early twenties, your personal development (education) and career/business/professional development may be at the top of your list. If you are in your mid-forties, finances, family, and relationships could be at the top. As you approach sixty, your health and fitness may be higher on your list. How you prioritize your list will change throughout your life.

When I was in my twenties, I believed I was immortal. I didn't worry about my health. I ate what I wanted, drank a lot of beer every weekend and smoked a twenty-pack of cigarettes daily. Health and fitness were pretty low down my list of areas of focus.

For those of you who like a drink or two on a weekend, you will have noticed around the age of thirty-five (and if you're not there yet, you have this to look forward to), hangovers from a night extensively exercising your drinking arm take two or three days to shake off. Around that time, health is likely to begin shooting up your list of priorities.

When we are young, free and single, we probably spend a large portion of our income on our social life (and image towards attractive people). If we get married and have children, building a financial safety net around our family is could rise rapidly up our list of priorities (hence the rapid rise in "dad bods" – they've got "the one," and they are no longer playing the market)

In middle school, education and friendships will have been high on your list of priorities, even though you were probably not aware of it at the time.

Wherever you are in life, your areas of focus will be prioritized towards what's most important to you *right now*.

Let's look at these areas individually to get a greater understanding of what each means. As you read through these eight areas, think about what you could do either daily, weekly, or monthly that would help you to meet your needs in these areas. For example, you may wish to spend ten minutes each day doing meditation, or perhaps dedicating an evening during the week as a family night. All of these activities will require time, but time spent here will be time spent in areas of your life that you have identified as being important to you.

Family and Relationships

This is about time spent with your family, making sure you care for those important to you and being there for them; spending enough time with your partner, children and parents. It should go without saying that your family and friends are important but given how important this area is, how much of your time and attention do you spend in this area?

Where you can improve here is how much time you spend with your family and friends. To do that, you will want to schedule time each week with your family or if you live a long way from your parents, ensuring you call them frequently. And likewise with your friends, having time to spend with them and to stay in touch. Not doing so will inevitably lead to you squeezing this area dry. It's easy to feel our family and friends will always be there for us – we tend to take them for granted. I hope, deep down, that is not the case.

We lose friendships not because we see too much of our friends but because we drift apart. Why? Because we allow our work and other low-priority tasks to get in the way. We fall into the trap of constantly dealing with the latest and loudest, believing we will have time to call or meet with them "one day." What does "one day" mean? Would it not be better to define it, so you don't drift apart?

Friendships, like marriage, take effort. Friendships need to be actively worked on to stay alive and fresh. When we neglect them, our friendships and relationships with our partners begin to wither and die. So, what can you do to keep your relationships and friendships alive? The answer to that question becomes an activity in your task manager or calendar.

Career/Business

What do you want from your career? Are you on track to achieve the position you want? Or, if your goal is to build your own business, are you doing everything you can do to accomplish that?

To reach an executive level within your company, what skills and professional qualifications do you need? Turning up at work daily and going through the motions will not get you where you want to be. Instead, taking consistent, positive action each day is the only vehicle enabling you to arrive where you want to be with your career.

Ask the most successful people in your organization how they arrived at their position , and the chances are they will tell you: hard work and persistence. They are focused on their long-term aspirations and ensure that what they do each day develops their skills.

knowledge, and reputation. Work is not "work" to them; it is part of a mission. They continue their mission every day. And, like all successful missions, there is a clear plan of action to follow.

When you have a clear mission for your career, you will be focused. You will see your work as important, and you will do whatever you can to ensure you complete your mission.

Leadership expert and author Robin Sharma often talks about visiting a bathroom when he was passing through Johannesburg Airport. In the bathroom was an attendant, and as Robin was leaving, he commented on how clean the bathroom was. The attendant turned to Robin with a huge, proud smile and told him that his "mission" was to have the cleanest airport toilet in the world! With that kind of dedication to a mission, you know that attendant bounced into work each day, ready to make sure he succeeded.

Perhaps it's the changing attitudes to work. In the past, work was not just about earning a living – it was also a vocation. A way to pass time and give us a sense of purpose constructively. Yet we rarely hear the word "vocation" today, and with few exceptions, it's unlikely people define their purpose from the work they do each day. And that may be why so many feel burnt out, depressed and tired.

Yet, if you spoke with that cleaner at Johannesburg Airport, you would feel something special, a sense of purpose and pride. That began with understanding what his work meant to him and why he was doing what he was doing.

When it comes to your professional life, what is *your* mission?

A financial advisor may see their mission to help people build an iron-clad fence of financial security around families; a farmer's mission might be to put food on people's tables. What you will find is if your mission at work is centered on serving others, you will have more enthusiasm and energy for your work than if your motives were financial or status.

Finances

A common cause of stress for most people is personal finance, or lack of it. The good news about personal finance is that as long as you have a regular savings plan and contribute to a retirement fund, the rest will mostly take care of itself – I know, sounds simple, but hear me out. Life is not a straight line where everything works as planned; if it were, life would be incredibly boring. There will be times when things are difficult. Perhaps you lose your job, or you need to find a significant amount of money for a medical emergency or procedure. Having your finances under control is not a short-term goal; it's a long-term plan.

Personal finance may seem difficult at times, but a simple strategy with a recurring task reminding you to send money to your savings account can do wonders for this potentially stressful area of life. When things are sound, and you have a job that pays you adequately, you may be able to send a little extra to your savings. When times are tough and the economy is unpredictable, you may want to reduce the amount you are saving for a while. Perhaps working on the principle of 1>0, i.e., putting $1.00 away is better than nothing at all.

This is not about the *amount* you put away each month; it's about developing the *habit* of putting something away each month. When we begin our professional journey, our starting salaries are typically low. It's difficult to pay a significant amount of your income into a savings account. However, even if we only put $5 or $10 away each month to begin with, you are developing a habit that, over time, will reward you immeasurably.

My wife is not a natural saver; she's more of a spender. However, a genius – well, a genius in my eyes – at her bank pointed her towards a pet saving scheme, where you put a given amount of money away each month into an account dedicated to your pet (in our case, our dog). She began that scheme ten years before our beloved Barney passed away in 2021, and at the end of it, Barney had "saved" $30,000!

That shocked my wife. She'd never saved anything in her life before. So, when our current dog, Louis, arrived, the first thing she did was go to the bank and open another pet savings account in the name of Louis. My wife frequently reminds me that Louis now has $6,000 saved, and he's only two years old!

Saving money is a habit and one well worth developing to give you that peace of mind to know you have something put aside in case things go catastrophically wrong.

Your financial future is vital to living without stress and anxiety. The sooner you start putting money away and saving for your future, the easier it will be.

Securing your financial area will only be achieved if you take action weekly and monthly. Planning your long-term financial future can easily be neglected, but having a recurring task each week or month reminding you to take action will keep this area of your life under control.

Health and Fitness

Health and fitness are among the most neglected areas of any person's life. Yet, you know these are important and become increasingly so as you age. Putting an exercise schedule in place could stave off long-term health issues and provide you with unbelievable energy and vitality.

The problem with the health and fitness area is it often gets relegated to the bottom of the list because it is hard. It's hard to get out of bed and go to the gym or come home from an exhausting day at the office and run.

However, exercise does not mean you need to join a gym or become a runner. These ideas are relatively new.

> If you look at pictures of people from the 1940s and 1950s, you will notice something immediately: relatively few people were overweight [*Source: https://www.nydailynews.com/2020/07/02/summer-in-new-york-1930s-to-1950s/*].
>
> Now, there are a multitude of reasons why that was the case, but one of the interesting things is there were no gyms or exercise classes like we have today. The biggest difference was that people walked a lot more than we do today. They moved. That is what you were designed to do: move.
>
> So, if you want to improve your overall fitness and health, move more.

Exercise means movement. You were not designed to spend eight hours or more sitting at a desk eating refined, processed foods and drinking sugary drinks. You were designed to move. Daily walking and using stairs whenever possible is one way to maintain your health and fitness.

Charles Darwin, author of The Origins of Species, would take two walks a day. His first was early in the morning and the second in the mid-afternoon. It became a part of his daily routine and was not only about health; it was also a time for him to gather his thoughts and think through complex scientific problems.

One trick you could use is to do some cleaning between sessions of work. For example, wash your tea and coffee mugs in one break or go outside and water your plants in another. Doing laundry, vacuuming your home office, and other chores can also be done if you work from home.

If you want to get on top of your health, there are three areas to focus on – sleep, diet and movement. If you get between six and eight hours of sleep each night, eat healthy, unrefined, or natural foods, and avoid sugar, you will see huge benefits to your overall productivity. Add a couple of thirty-minute walks, and you will be well on your way to keeping your health and fitness area in check.

If you don't know how much sleep you need, do an experiment and sleep with no alarm for seven days. Note how much sleep you get each night and average it out. That will tell you how much sleep you naturally need. We are all different here.

Getting enough sleep each day will radically improve your overall productivity and mood, so you are a lot more attentive to the people you care about.

Now, what about exercise? Now, here's the problem with exercise: a lot of people hate exercise. Possibly because of how they were introduced to exercise at school, which has left a scar that still lives with them today. Yet exercise is essential for productivity.

What is involved in movement or activity? A thirty-minute intentional walk would do. But you can go further. Stop using elevators or escalators. Reintroduce yourself to the stairs. Stairs are an excellent source for getting the blood flowing and improving your focus and productivity.

(The usual caveats apply here. If you have not exercised for a long time or have any underlying illnesses, do, please check with your doctor first.)

Seventy years ago there wasn't the convenience we have today. Escalators were rare; very few people had televisions in their homes (and those that did had to keep getting up to change the channel), and if someone called you, you again had to get up, go to the hall and answer the phone.

There was no home delivery pizza and fewer convenience foods, so we had to cook. Our whole lives were based around movement.

Today, it's perfectly normal for people to get home, sit on the sofa and not move again until they head off to bed four or five hours later. They leave their homes, walk a few meters to their car, drive to the office, park in the car park, walk a few meters to the elevator, go to their desks, and spend the next eight or nine hours sitting down. Then repeat the homeward journey to spend the evening sitting on a sofa.

Is it any wonder in the developed world, it is estimated that by 2030 over 60% of people will be dangerously overweight and either in the early stages of or have some form of preventable metabolic disease? [Source: https://www.ajpmonline.org/article/s0749-3797(12)00146-8/fulltext#figures]

If you're not getting enough sleep or exercise and your diet is a disaster zone, that is a big part of the reason why you are stressed out, overwhelmed, and tired all the time. It's not your work or the things you have to do.

How much time could you dedicate each day to sleep and movement? Could you commit to getting seven hours of sleep and spending forty minutes moving each day?

Making changes in these three areas of your life: your sleep, movement, and diet, will have a profound impact on your energy levels throughout the day, which will impact the quality and quantity not only of what you do at work but with your relationships with the people that matter most to you.

Plus, of course, you will significantly reduce your risk of developing debilitating lifestyle diseases that ultimately prevent you from living the life you have always dreamed of.

Spirituality

This area involves everyone, no matter what your religion or beliefs. Your spirituality could mean you find time each week to go to church, temple, synagogue, or mosque, or it may simply mean you get outside and spend some time in nature away from all the digital demands on your everyday life.

The time you have away and being alone will do wonders for your overall mental health and wellbeing. At a minimum, you might try spending a few minutes each day meditating or relaxing in peace and quiet.

I've always struggled with meditation. I like the idea, but it's never worked for me. Instead, I discovered the spiritual philosopher Alan Watts and will listen to his teachings for twenty minutes or so most evenings.

Over the years, I've had the pleasure of meeting people who wake up early to attend their synagogue or to visit their local temple at 5:00 am. For many, it's a fantastic way to start the day. It can balance you spiritually and brings some structure to your day. It is about discovering you are part of a greater power and that there is more to life than a job and a salary.

Spirituality is about bringing some perspective into our lives. Whether studying the Quran, Torah or Bible, the teachings help us understand life, its meaning and how we can be better people. Even if you are not religious, these books are some of the best self-help books ever written.

Another way to help you connect to your inner voice is to write a journal. Journaling is a way to express yourself, your thoughts, and to ask yourself deep questions about your life. It helps to slow your mind and get you away from the hustle and bustle of everyday life. And, a journal is a great way to keep track of how you are improving as the years go by.

Spirituality is an important area to help keep you grounded and at one with yourself.

Lifestyle and Life Experiences

This area likely needs no introduction. This area involves the *things you possess*. It may seem shallow to want material things, but we are humans, and, for most, there's always something we would like to have in our lives. Whether you dream of owning a Rolls-Royce or a Ferrari or designing and building your own home, these are worthy dreams. They can inspire us and bring a sense of excitement. Life should never be only about our work. Enjoying the fruits of your labor is essential, so having a few material wants is not necessarily bad.

Material things can also be a healthy distraction, from restoring a classic car to building a miniature railway in your attic. Both activities can be expensive yet might help you to balance your life between your professional duties and your personal pleasures.

During the UK's austere years of the 1950s, families dreamed of owning a car, travelling abroad for a holiday, or purchasing a television. These were aspirational purchases, and people worked and saved hard to have them. There were fewer luxury goods to buy, but people still dreamed of owning material things. These dreams are an inbuilt human instinct; you shouldn't feel ashamed of them. Instead, use them to inspire and energize you.

Life experiences, the places you visit, and where you go on your vacations are all important and need to be a part of your life. Our lives are built on the experiences we have. Do you have a place-to-visit list? This is one of the best lists you can keep in your notes (or journal). Each year, you can look at this list and consider one of those places as a possible vacation destination that year.

"Life is about experience... you can't hold onto everything." – Sarah Addison Allen

Personal Development

It is a mistake to believe that once your formal education ends, that's it. The reality is that it's just the beginning. It's now up to you to build on those foundations, whether through university education or using those skills as a platform to achieve greater things.

You should always have one skill you are developing at any time. That could be learning a foreign language, a musical instrument, or a piece of software. These skills will allow you to keep growing and increase your creativity throughout life. Perhaps there were courses or subjects you wanted to learn at school but were unable to do so. Why not do it now?

What are you interested in, and would like to take a course in? The digital world has opened up new opportunities for you to learn almost anything you want.

Personal development can also be about the books you read. Biographies, history, and special interest topics are great ways to develop yourself.

Find something you are curious about and dig deeper. The more you read, the more you will develop your skills because you don't just learn from your mistakes; you can learn a lot from the mistakes of others.

Purpose in Life

This one will likely be the hardest area to define. Most people do not know what their purpose in life is until they reach their thirties or forties or older. The one thing I've learned about purpose in life is that we are likely already working towards it – we just haven't externalized it yet.

> "Don't feel guilty if you don't know what you want to do with your life...the most interesting people I know didn't know at 22 what they wanted to do with their lives, some of the most interesting 40-year-olds I know still don't."
>
> - From the song, *Everybody's Free (To Wear Sunscreen)* by Baz Luhrmann

I spent most of my twenties without a clue about my purpose. But one thing that has been with me for years – probably from when I was a teenager – is that I love teaching new things to people. It was only when I became a teacher at thirty that it became clear that my purpose in life was to teach people ways to improve their lives. Looking back now, I can guess this purpose came from my curiosity about the lives of successful people. Learning from the likes of Nelson Mandela, Mohammed Ali, Sebastian Coe, and Ian Fleming inspired me at an early age, and have had a compulsion to tell everyone about what I have learned from these amazing people.

So, if you don't yet know your purpose, don't worry. It will come once you start thinking about it. Reminisce about your past, what you enjoyed at school and early life; there will likely be clues there. What were you interested in then that still interests you today?

There are a few questions you can ask yourself that may help you find your purpose:

- Why did you choose the career you are in?
- What books do you like to read?
- What articles are you drawn to in the newspaper?
- What videos do you find yourself watching a lot on YouTube or elsewhere?

From your answers, ask yourself *why*.

The way to build out your areas of focus is first to establish what each one means to you by writing out a statement. Let's look at what a clarifying statement would look like for each of the eight categories; this is just a sample. You will want to define what each area means to you. The more personal you can make it, the more powerful each will be. This is about how you see yourself – your internal identity, if you like – and when your daily actions and activities match your inner identity, that's when you experience balance.

Family and Relationships – *I provide a loving, caring and financially stable environment for my family and friends and ensure I always make time for them whenever they need my help and support.*

Career and Business – *I work hard and do my work to the best of my abilities. I do not engage in office gossip and treat my colleagues, customers, and suppliers. respectfully. My ultimate goal is to build my own company, and I will use my time as an employee to learn, grow and develop my skills.*

Health and Fitness – *I am fit and healthy, and exercise regularly. I am careful about what I eat and monitor my health frequently. I maintain my weight at around 80 KG and my body fat percentage at less than 20%.*

Spirituality – *I am mindful of my life. I meditate every morning to bring calm and peace into my world, and I thank my creator every day for the beautiful life I have.*

Personal Development – *I practice self-development every day. I read quality articles, books, and other materials to learn from others, and practice new skills, so I am a constant work in progress. I learn from my mistakes and the successes and mistakes of others.*

Lifestyle and Life Experiences – *Every month, I experience something new. That could be trying a new activity, travelling to a new place, or doing something* *entirely out of character. I maintain a list of new things to try, do and visit, and will complete at least three things from my bucket list every year.*

Finances – *I save a minimum of $100.00 each month. I am careful how I spend my money, seeking investment, not consumption. I ensure I contribute to my pension and manage the risk in my investments.*

Purpose in Life – *I will help as many people as possible become better organized and more productive. I help people become less stressed and to focus on spending more time doing what they want. I will always have time to help people develop themselves and grow their careers and businesses. My whole purpose is to help people. It energizes me every day, and that is why I wake up every morning.*

In Benjamin Franklin's autobiography, he described the virtues he considered important:

1. TEMPERANCE. Eat not to dullness; drink not to elevation.

2. SILENCE. Speak not but what may benefit others or yourself; avoid trifling conversation.

3. ORDER. Let all your things have their places; let each part of your business have its time.

4. RESOLUTION. Resolve to perform what you ought; perform without fail what you resolve.

5. FRUGALITY. Make no expense but to do good to others or yourself; i.e., waste nothing.

6. INDUSTRY. Lose no time; be always employ'd in something useful; cut off all unnecessary actions.

7. SINCERITY. Use no hurtful deceit; think innocently and justly, and, if you speak, speak accordingly.

8. JUSTICE. Wrong none by doing injuries, or omitting the benefits that are your duty.

9. MODERATION. Avoid extreams; forbear resenting injuries so much as you think they deserve.

10. CLEANLINESS. Tolerate no uncleanliness in body, cloaths, or habitation.

11. TRANQUILLITY. Be not disturbed at trifles, or at accidents common or unavoidable.

12. CHASTITY. Rarely use venery but for health or offspring, never to dullness, weakness, or the injury of your own or another's peace or reputation.

13. 13. HUMILITY. Imitate Jesus and Socrates.

Notice how he defined each one with a simple sentence. This is what you are looking to do when writing out your areas of focus, defining what they mean to you.

The more emotion you can bring to these statements, the better they will be. Use adjectives to spice them up and make them uniquely personal for you. Keep in mind you will only be sharing these with yourself, so they need to inspire you.

For example, you could use words like:

- Outstanding set of skills / Outstanding sister, brother, parent.

- Olympic champion levels of fitness.

- Sponge for knowledge.

- A beacon of calmness.

Turning Areas Into Tasks

One of the tools you will learn about shortly is the task manager. This tool is where you will put the things you want or need to do each day. In this next exercise, I am going to ask you to pull out the actions (tasks) that will mean you are consistently doing the things you need to do to stay in balance with these areas. For now, I would suggest you write down the actions you can take to maintain this balance.

What you will notice from these examples is most of them are measurable, such as doing something new each month as part of your *life experiences* area or maintaining your weight at around 80kg. These are easily monitored by having a monthly recurring task that reminds you to take a weight reading each month or plan a trip at the beginning of the month with your partner or friends.

Making these statements measurable ensures you can monitor your progress, and they continue to move you towards becoming the person you want to be.

Once you have a meaningful statement written out for each area, you go through each one, looking for actions you can take to ensure you remain focused on them.

For instance, with the *family and relationships* example above, you may have something like "always being aware of the needs of those around me and calling my parents once a week."

In this instance, you cannot turn "being aware of the needs of others around you" into a task, but calling your parents once a week can be converted to a task that would be transferred to your *recurring areas of focus* section in your to-do list manager.

You may also have something like "save $100.00 each month for a rainy day" in your financial area. What would you need to do to ensure you do this each month? Perhaps you could add a recurring task (a task that repeats on a given day each month) to your task manager that says: "Send $100.00 to my Rainy Day Fund." That task will now appear on the given date each month to remind you to do it.

In your *health and fitness* area, you might have the following action steps associated with this area:

- Exercise a minimum of 4 times per week.

- Do 16:8 intermittent fasting 5 days per week.

- Drink lemon juice water every morning.

- Take my vitamins and supplements every day.

With exercise a minimum of four times per week, that would be an item you put on your calendar. Exercise is not a task; it is an event. You need to be at a specific place at a particular time. You either need to go to the gym, a class, go walking or running.

You would put intermittent fasting on your calendar as an all-day event to remind you that you will be doing an intermittent fasting session on that day.

Drinking your lemon juice water and taking your vitamins could become a part of your morning and evening routines; for that, you could have a checklist. (More on those later in this book)

The idea is you take these action steps and either get them on your calendar or, if they are identifiable tasks that need doing such as sending an amount of money to your savings account each month, you would add them as a task to your recurring areas of focus section in your task manager.

When we look at goal setting, you will notice many of the activities and action steps you identify will come from your areas of focus tasks. It's natural that your long-term goals and your areas of focus will interconnect on some levels.

For instance, if one of your long-term goals is to have the freedom to travel the world when you finally stop working, building enough of a financial base to allow you to do that would be important. That will come under your finance areas of focus. If you want to enjoy exploring the places you visit as you travel the world, taking care of your health and fitness would be important, because if you do not have good health when you do have the resources and time to travel the world, it won't matter. You would not be able to be free to explore all the fantastic places you dreamt of visiting. So, making sure your health is in balance would also come into the mix.

Projects and Goals Will Always Start At An Area of Focus Level

All your meaningful projects and goals will ultimately begin at your areas of focus level. Your work projects will begin from your career/business area of focus and will likely cross over to your personal development area.

If you look at your job as something you hate but something you have to do each day, you are not going to gain anything from the experience except a paycheck. However, if you flip that thinking and treat your current job and role as education, you will have a far better experience, and it will be as if you are being paid to learn and grow. Now that's a huge win!

> *What did you learn from your first job?*
>
> Think back to your first job, whether that was a part-time school holiday job or the first job you had on your career journey. What were three things you learned? (Flipping hamburgers and knowing how to professionally detail a car count!)

In every job you have had in the past, you will have learned something valuable. Treat every new job as an education.

An interesting thing you will begin to notice is any project or goal you embark on that you eventually lose interest in will be something that does not relate to any of your areas of focus. The reason is that ultimately, whenever you have a project or goal that does not serve a higher purpose in your life, you won't have the motivation to carry it through to the end because your motivation will fizzle out. Work projects will be different because there will be other people holding you to account to do your job (your relationships area of focus), and as a successfully completed project will look good on your resume, it will also link back to your career and business area.

The happiest, most fulfilled people I know all work from their goals and areas of focus. Everything they do comes from these.

Working from your areas of focus will help you build a time management and productivity system that leaves you feeling energized and fulfilled, knowing you are always doing something meaningful and important to *you* instead of seeing time management as something you only associate with your work.

That's what a purpose-built personal productivity and time management system does. You no longer find yourself switching between apps and looking for something new in which to dump all those meaningless tasks. You focus more on what's really important to you. Each day, you will be moving the needle closer towards the life you want to live, and doing more of the things you want to do.

It all starts with knowing what it is you want. If you do not know this, your whole task management system will fill up with other people's tasks. You will be the person to whom other people delegate their less meaningful tasks and that means you lose control of your time.

That changes when you know what you want. Your work tasks become opportunities to learn and grow (personal development). Client or customer problems become chances for you to show what you can do.

Homework

Spend some time over the next few days and think about your areas of focus within the eight areas. Create your own "mission statement" for each one, and make sure your statements mean something to you. Avoid generic phrases and ensure what you write is measurable, or at the very least, you will be able to monitor your progress.

Once you have your statements written, pull out what action steps you need to take and put them into your calendar as recurring events or tasks in your task manager.

When it comes to getting organized and improving time management and productivity, this is one vital part of the process that most people will skip, believing that doing it is a luxury they don't have time for. There's a reason you don't have time to do it. Not knowing what you want and what is important to you means you end up focused on other people's priorities and neglecting your life (time does not like a vacuum). This can be debilitating to your mental and physical health in the long term and it means you "don't have time" for anything you want to do.

When you decide to get yourself organized and in control of your time, it is important to clear the decks, and that means before you start, you clear what you currently have ongoing. That does not mean you continue to accept new tasks and commitments. It means you draw a line on any new inputs and clear the backlog. This is important because you want to have a clear mind for working on yourself and your priorities.

If you've ever seen an old building demolished so a new one can be built, you may have noticed every last trace of the old building is removed before the foundations are set for the new building. Not doing so would mean compromises would need to be made in order to build the new building.

To do this, it's best to take a few days off. Get away from Slack, Teams, email, and any other source of work and change your environment. Book yourself in a boutique hotel in the countryside or perhaps on the coast if you can. Alternatively, find a quiet coffee shop or cafe where you can go and be undisturbed for a few hours. This change in environment will stimulate your creativity and thought process.

Author and entrepreneur Tim Ferriss, and Microsoft founder, Bill Gates regularly take a week off and "disappear" to focus on their thoughts and recharge themselves. Not in a family holiday way, rather in a more solitary manner. Family holidays can often be as stressful, if not more so, than being at work.

Once you are in a new environment, think about what you want out of life, your long-term goals, what you would like to be doing in ten or twenty years, and how you want to live your life today. Go through every part of your life and ask yourself if you are happy with it. If not, what could you do to change things and be happy? Write down the results of your thinking.

> *Get out and walk.* Walking does something wonderfully chemical to your brain and releases some naturally occurring super-drugs into your bloodstream that will aid you in thinking about what you want. It isn't a coincidence that Isaac Newton discovered gravity while walking outside (although it did hit him on the head while he was sitting underneath an apple tree).

Knowing what you want is where you start building a productivity and time management system that will serve you now and long into the future. It is the things you need to do to achieve the life you want that you prioritize each day.

Life coach Tony Robbins has a productivity system called RPM (Rapid Planning Method), which is a phenomenal system. I would argue it is one of the best systems you could adopt. However, 95% of those who learn about this method will never implement it because it takes a lot of time to put all the pieces in place.

RPM does not focus on all the noise around you today. Instead, it forces you to think about what you want and what is important to you based on the categories you wish to focus your life on.

The desire for instant gratification will always tend to destroy your long-term productivity because you will never do the back-end work needed to ensure what you are doing each day is serving you and not just serving those around you. You want to be building your day around *your* priorities and then allowing time to deal with everyone else's.

A typical day when you spend time focused on the right things might mean starting the day with an hour dedicated to yourself. That could involve some light exercise, meditation, journal writing or something mentally nourishing. Then you begin your day with a family breakfast where you are focused on your family (not your email or phone).

Each morning when you begin work, you know your priorities because you planned for the day the night before. You can get straight to it, focusing on doing your best work .

When your work for the day is over, you may have a family dinner or dinner with a friend before returning home and reading, or talking with your family and friends.

If you have done the hard work of establishing what is important to you, all these activities will fall into place, and while you do them, you will feel focused, motivated, and fulfilled because what you are doing is moving you forward. You are improving by 1% each day. That sense of growth generates motivation and the all-important momentum.

The steps to establishing a fulfilled and happy life are simple. The difficulty is doing the hard back-end work. But I can promise you, if you do decide to take those few days to go deep and learn what you want out of life, you will never regret it. You will be more motivated, energized, and happier because you will see each new day as a step toward becoming the person you want to become.

The alternative is more stress, more overwhelm, and a tragically unhappy life. Always remember, nothing will ever change unless you change. So what do you have to lose?

> *You are not going to have "perfect" days every day.* Doing the homework I have set for you in this book will not guarantee perfection. You are human with feelings and emotions. You're going to have bad days. Celebrate these; it's confirmation there is nothing wrong with you.

You may have a fight with your partner, one of your children could be "troublesome," or you may have a teenager in the house. These and many other external forces will affect how you feel each day. Remember, you are not building a time/life management system for just one day. You're building a system for life. Embrace the bad days, do what you can and move on to the next day.

As the Stoics would say "*Amor Fati*" – love your fate.

We have now dealt with your areas of focus. You have the first foundation of a solid and inspiring time management system.

In the next chapter, we will examine the different types of tools you can use to enhance your time management and productivity.

4

The Tools You Will Need

"It is essential to have good tools, but it is also essential that the tools should be used in the right way." – Wallace D. Wattles

I have already alluded to using a task manager and notes app, but you are also going to find a calendar helpful. I like to think of these as the tools that will assist you in becoming better organized and more productive. And just like a craftsperson carrying a toolbox wherever they go and do their work, you too will carry with you a toolbox of productivity tools that will serve you for many years to come.

Paper or Digital?

Let's deal with a question I am frequently asked: which is better: paper or digital tools?

Digital tools give you greater flexibility, and you have less to carry. Paper is great, and for a lot of people, paper works better for brainstorming ideas and outlining a plan. Paper systems are also cheap and don't crash or stop functioning.

Pen and paper are also excellent at encouraging you to think deeper, and you're not going to get notifications jumping out from the page every few minutes interrupting your thoughts.

However, there are some disadvantages to using paper. The biggest is storage. Over time, you are going to build up a lot of notes and task lists, and you will want to be able to keep these accessible wherever you are. Notebooks fill up and have to be stored somewhere. Five or six notebooks are easy to store, but when you start building up twenty, thirty or forty or more notebooks, things get difficult. You also have the disadvantage of only carrying with you your current notes and tasks. There will be occasions where you may need to refer to a meeting note from last year or some project plans you made two years ago, and it will be difficult and slow to find these items.

When you organize everything in digital tools, all your notes, projects, and tasks are searchable. It does not matter where you are. You could be on the other side of the world, and as long as you have one of your digital devices with you and an internet connection, you will be able to access your notes. My advice is to choose digital tools.

This does not mean you shouldn't use paper ever. You may find when planning out a project or seeking a solution to a difficult problem, the best thing to do is to open a paper notebook, and with a few different colored pens (and some highlighters if you want some extra fun), brainstorm ideas. Paper is fantastic for this because you see everything you write in one place. If you were to do this digitally, as your notes grow you will need to scroll up and down just to see what you previously wrote.

If you do use paper, once you have finished brainstorming you could scan the paper note into your digital notes. This way you will always have a searchable copy of your initial ideas in your digital system.

A Calendar

This is going to be important because later in this book, you will learn how to use *time blocking*, and a calendar will enable you to do that. You will want to be able to move blocks around and add appointments on the fly.

Your calendar will prove to be your most important tool as this is the only tool you have that will tell you whether you have time to do something or not. Your calendar does not lie to you. It has twenty-four hours each day, and you cannot change that. That's all you have each day, and despite wishing for more, that is something you are never going to be able to change, sorry! Your calendar will tell you if you have time to work on a project today and where you need to be at 3 pm. It will tell you when you need to pick up your kids from their judo or ballet class on Thursday and when your football team is playing their next game.

The best thing about your calendar is you can schedule a time to get all your work done, and once you have done that, you will feel a lot less stressed because you know you have time to complete your work. It also allows you to say "no" more confidently. If you are asked to do something, all you need do is say, "Let me check my calendar and get back to you," and you have a simple yet effective way of avoiding being pushed into committing to do something you do not want to do.

> A trick I learned several years ago was before accepting any new appointment or meeting, instead of immediately saying yes – even if you know you can do it – always say, "Let me check my calendar and get back to you."

> While this does add an additional task in that you will need to confirm or decline the invitation, it gives both of you time to make a decision about the value of the meeting or appointment. The meetings I wanted to attend were easy to confirm, and those meetings I was skeptical about I could politely decline on the basis my diary was full.

A Notes Application

Your Notes app will be the backbone of your whole system. This is where all your project notes and links to files will go. It is also where your long-term goals, areas of focus statements and checklists will be kept.

Of all the digital productivity tools that have grown over the last few years, it's perhaps the notes app that has been the most useful. After all, calendars and to-do lists were never really a problem. Diaries were easily carried around in a pocket, and you could use your calendar or Post-It Notes for to-dos.

The area that was more difficult was notes because it was hard to carry notebooks around with us, and even if we did that, there was the issue of having disorganized notes all over the place. Digital notes apps give you the ability to keep everything in a single place, and with the search capabilities in these tools, it's now easier than ever to find what you are looking for.

I've been using a notes application called Evernote since 2009. Over the years, I have collected a lot of notes, articles, websites and more in there. I'm often amazed how I can simply type in a keyword into the search box – even a vague idea of one – and Evernote will give me the results from as far back as 2009 in less than a second.

Meeting notes from ten years ago can be found simply by searching for the year I think the meeting was and a keyword, be that a person, a topic, or a location.

Your notes application is also where you will keep your master projects list. This list is a single note that gives you an overview of your current projects – both personal and work-related – and it is also the best place to plan out your projects and goals as well as what you will work on in which quarter.

Many years ago, in the pre-digital age, our offices and homes had a strange piece of furniture called a filing cabinet. These were rectangle metal cabinets, usually in a boring cream or grey color, that were filled with project and client files, important documents related to insurance, cars, and finances, and a lot of other things like receipts, guarantees and user manuals for all the devices we had. They were lockable and when full of stuff – which they quickly became – very heavy. You couldn't exactly walk out of a building carrying one of these.

Today, a digital notes app can hold all that stuff and a lot more and be carried with you on a handheld smartphone wherever you go.

That alone is the biggest advantage of having a digital notes app. Everything you need to do your work is with you wherever you go.

If you have not used a digital notes app before, Apple's Notes and Microsoft's OneNote are great places to start. There are a number of third-party notes apps such as the previously mentioned Evernote as well as Notion and Obsidian.

A Task Manager

In essence, a "task manager" is a to-do list. This is quite different from a "project manager." A project manager is a complex piece of software designed to manage big projects such as building a large office block or a NASA space mission. These project managers are designed to be operated by many different departments, from the finance team, where they can monitor the costs of a project, to the procurement team, who needs to know what to purchase and when so that the right materials are where they need to be when they need to be there.

I have seen a lot of people try to use these project managers as task managers and quickly find themselves overwhelmed by all the stuff they put in there just to make it appear functional. Avoid this mistake at all costs! You are building a "personal" productivity system, which means you do not need all those collaboration tools, financial reports, and client requisition areas.

A task manager is a lot simpler. It is a place where you can collect all your tasks, commitments, and to-dos into a single inbox so you can process these into a set of lists or folders at the end of the day and decide what needs to be done and when you will do it. If managed properly, your task manager will do the hard work of sorting out what tasks you should be working on today.

Your task manager needs to be simple because, ultimately, *the less time you spend there, the more time you will have to do your work.* If your task manager is complex with a lot of features, you will spend far too much time tagging, labelling, thinking about where to put a task and reorganizing your many lists. That is *not* being productive. Doing the right things at the right time *is* being productive. You need your task manager to be simple, so the only thing to think about is what a task is, what will be required to complete the task and when you will do the task.

During the day, your task manager is there to keep you focused on what you have prioritized that day and acts as a place for you to collect tasks and commitments as they pop up. You should avoid allowing it to become a covert distraction that pulls you away from doing the work you need to get done while fooling you into thinking you are doing something productive by reorganizing your lists and reviewing all your tasks.

Reviewing is not doing!

> If you're starting out with a task manager, try the built-in ones on your computer. Microsoft's ToDo is excellent as is Apple's Reminders. Google tasks is very simple, and you can connect that to your Google Calendar.
>
> There are a lot of third-party task managers too that are worth looking into if the above don't appeal to you.

Cloud Storage

When personal computers began to take off in the mid to late 1990s, software developers believed we would naturally be able to manage our documents and files ourselves. After all, we had been using filing cabinets for well over a century. People didn't leave their insurance, car registration documents, bank statements and birthday/marriage certificates lying around on the kitchen dining table for all to see. They put them away in a place where they could be found when needed.

For some strange reason, we stopped doing that with personal computers. We left important documents on the desktop, which meant we wasted a lot of time just trying to find things. We were told in countless articles that leaving stuff on your desktop slowed your computer down, and you risked losing everything if your computer died (which in the late 1990s and early 2000s they often did – remember the "blue screen of death"?)

Around 2005, software companies and engineers realized we were not going to listen, and so began the growth of cloud storage systems. These promised that if we filed our important documents away into the cloud, they would be safe, and if our computers did die, there was always a backup. Companies like Dropbox gave us a way to store our important documents safely. Soon, Google, Microsoft and Apple followed (although Apple had introduced something like this in the early 2000s called .Mac, which later became MobileMe) .

With the improvements in computer systems search, cloud computing has become an excellent way to keep documents, PDFs, and copies of important documents such as your insurance certificates, birth certificates and driver's licenses. As long as you clearly name the file, you have almost instant access to any file kept in the cloud from any of your devices.

With cloud storage, I recommend you use your computer's system. For instance, if all your devices are in Apple's ecosystem, Apple's own iCloud will work best for you. If you work predominantly in Google's ecosystem, use Google Drive, and similarly with Windows, Microsoft's OneDrive is excellent.

Third-party cloud storage systems like Dropbox work well if you have devices on multiple platforms. Dropbox is available on all mobile systems as well as desktops. Google Drive and Microsoft OneDrive are also available on all devices.

Cloud storage security

No online cloud storage system will ever be totally secure. If you are worried about whether your information could be read by others, the only secure option is the store all your documents and files on an external drive that you never connect to when your computer has access to the internet. Of course, the risk of loss or damage to that drive is a tradeoff.

I advise using two-factor authentication, which means before a new device can access your files, you will typically be sent a text message with a code or password, or a personal digital key. Only by inputting that code will you be able to gain access. Of course, you should also use strong passwords and change those passwords frequently to protect your information.

Ultimately, this is for you to decide. Particularly sensitive documents, such as banking details, are best kept outside these online storage services. Many services will allow you to store important documents offline, which may be something you prefer. Just remember, if something is stored offline, you will not have access to it when not with the device that information is stored.

What To Think About When Selecting Your Tools

There are thousands of different apps on the market, all promising you that their app will be the answer to your productivity and time management problems. Let me tell you a secret: No app will ever make you more productive. The only thing that will make you more productive is *you*. To become more productive, you will need to become more effective at what YOU do. The right tools can help you, but they will not do it alone. Ultimately, to get your work done, you have to do the work.

With that said, the tools you use should work for the way you work. A mistake I see many people making is allowing themselves to be influenced by the latest trend or by a YouTuber who says they would not be able to get all their content produced without this tool (while conveniently forgetting to inform you they have a team of people producing the content for them).

Let me give you an example; at the time of writing this book, there is a current trend for notes apps called PKMs (Personal Knowledge Managers). These apps are notes apps with a fancy name that allow you to easily connect related notes together and show you the connections in nice charts. They look great and are very tempting. But before you jump on this bandwagon, you need to know if this kind of note app would work for the way you work.

You may like to see lists in a simple checklist or bullet list; you may also prefer to see graphics and images for more complex notes. An application such as the current breed of PKMs may not work well with the way you work because dropping an image or chart in a note is not simple. If you prefer to be able to create simple tables, use colors, and be able to drag and drop files and images into notes, a digital notes app such as OneNote or Apple Notes would work best.

If you come from an academic background, these new PKM apps work well because they are based on academic research tools. Just slightly simplified and with a few little shiny buttons to appeal to non-academic people.

Now, that's not to say these apps definitely wouldn't work for you. As with all apps, there will be a certain amount of compromise.

When choosing which tools to use, you will find the easiest one to decide on will be your calendar. There are three solid backend calendars to choose from: Google Calendar, Microsoft Outlook, or Apple Calendar.

All three of these calendar services work with other applications. For example, If you have an iPhone and a Windows computer, you can use the built-in calendar app on each device and just add your backend calendar's details. In other words, you subscribe to your own calendar. With your calendar, I would suggest you use the calendar service you are currently using.

Your task manager is more complicated. As with notes apps, there are thousands of different apps to choose from. These range from the very simple to the very complex. The best advice I can give you here is to avoid the more complex ones: they don't work any better than the simple ones, but they cost a lot more and have a lot more features that you probably don't need. The temptation to fiddle with these additional features will be high, so avoid them.

With your task manager, all you need is an app that supports folders or lists. The built-in task manager on an iPhone, Reminders, works well. You can create different lists, and you can bundle these up into folders. Likewise, with Microsoft's ToDo, you can create folders, and as long as you can do that, then the app will work.

If you prefer a more visual app, apps like Trello and Asana are great, but rather than creating folders, you create columns. It's a little more complex, but it can be made to work.

And that's it. As long as you have a calendar, a task manager, and a notes app, you are good to go.

It will take a little while to choose the right apps, and if you are new to the world of productivity and time management apps, you are going to go through a period of experimentation. Just remember, you will never find the perfect app. That does not exist. What you are looking for is a set of apps you enjoy using, show what you need to see in a clean, easy-to-read format, and work on all your devices.

Once you have found a set of apps you are reasonably happy with, stick with them. Don't be tempted to keep switching and trying new apps. That's a rabbit hole you do not want to go down. It creates a mess and can be one of the biggest destroyers of your productivity. Take pride in how long you have been using an app.

> I've been using Todoist for nine years, Evernote for fourteen, and Apple Calendar for 22 years. David Allen, author of *Getting Things Done*, has been using the same task management software for well over twenty years. That's something to be very proud of. It means you are focused on *doing*, not *playing*.

Give any new app you use at least six months of regular use. This gives you enough time to properly learn how to use the app and get used to the way your app works on the different devices you use.

I've often said the productivity apps you use need to be boring. This means they should disappear into the background but be there when you need them. You don't want to be tempted into constantly playing with features. They just need to work. To be more productive, you need to spend time doing the work you want to get done. Boring apps support that.

You'll also find that boring apps rarely go wrong. The worst thing you can do with time is waste it trying to figure out why an app won't do what it's supposed to do. I've wasted so much time in the past messing around in this area. The simpler the app, the less likely it will go wrong.

I should also warn you here about apps that claim to link different apps together. Common ones are apps such as IFTTT (If This Then That) or Zapiers. These apps allow you to connect your notes to your task manager or calendar to your task manager, for instance. When they work, they are fantastic. Unfortunately, they don't work perfectly.

From time to time, they will disconnect or stop working for some unknown reason. When that happens, you will not be aware of the disconnect immediately. All it takes is for one of these links to break just once, and you will stop trusting your system. When you lose trust in your system, you will return to trying to remember your commitments in your head – something I am going to try and stop you from doing in this book.

Homework

Now you know about the apps to use. In the next few chapters, we are going to set up your system. This means if you do not have a set of tools yet, now would be a good time to select some. Keep things simple for now; you can change your tools later. If you really don't know what to use, use whatever is already on your computer. That would be Microsoft ToDo and OneNote, or Apple Reminders and Apple Notes. You will find the next few chapters easier to go through if you already have chosen a calendar, task manager and notes app.

5

The Basics Of A Productivity System: Collect, Organize and Do (COD)

"Basically, I just relied on organization, personal checklists, and training so that I had my mind made up as to what I would do in the first sixty, ninety seconds of a crisis." – Gene Kranz
NASA Mission Control Flight Director, Apollo 11 and 13

About seven years ago, I was trying to think of a way to help people better understand the very basics of any great personal productivity system. This wasn't easy, because there were thousands of articles and books on creating personal productivity systems, all with conflicting advice. It was confusing, and I knew that those who only wanted to learn how to manage their work would likely give up the research as being too complex.

As I analyzed many of these materials and broke everything down into their component parts. I discovered that all of the systems I considered among the best had one thing in common, and that was three things underlying these systems:

- **Collect** stuff;

- **Organize** that stuff so it means something to you;

- **Do** the work; or,

COD. Collect, Organize, Do.

And that is how *COD* was born. I have taught these principles ever since, and the Time Sector System is built on these three foundational steps.

Collect

Collect means anything that comes your way that has your attention needs to be collected into a trusted place. As you now know, we have three places where we can put this stuff: your task manager, your notes, or your calendar. As stuff comes in, we can decide where best to put it. A task would go into your task manager, a meeting would go onto your calendar, and an idea would go into your notes app. That's reasonably straightforward, but "stuff" doesn't always conform to neat, tidy pockets.

Often, something could be considered an idea or a task. An idea, for instance, for a project you are currently working on could be a task or a note. When something like this comes in, it is not always clear where to put it. When this happens, it's easy to waste a lot of time trying to decide.

Primary Collection Tool

The solution to this is when something comes in you need to remember; the goal is to collect it, not necessarily make a decision about it right there. If something is obvious, for instance, a meeting appointment, then that can be put on your calendar, but if it is not obvious, you need to decide what your primary collection tool will be.

My primary collection tool is my task manager. It is by far the fastest way to get something into my system, and it was designed for simple and quick collection. I go through my task manager's inbox at the end of every day, and I am confident anything I throw in there will be dealt with within 24 hours.

I cannot say the same for my notes app. I rarely look at that at the end of the day, so I don't treat anything in there as urgent.

I find I will throw ideas and appointments that need confirming into my task manager because I can decide later what needs to be done with the input. I've often added things like: "Set up a meeting with Wendell next Tuesday" or "Arrange a call with Bill on Saturday AM" in my task manager. These don't really belong in my task manager, but they act as a reminder to transfer those appointments to my calendar when I clear my inbox at the end of the day.

Another reason for having a primary collection tool is to avoid having too many places to check at the end of the day. Many days, when you close down the day, you will be tired. You want to optimize the closing-down procedure so that it takes as little time as possible. If you have to check multiple inboxes, you are going to miss something important.

So, pick one primary tool, whether your notes or your task manager, and nominate that as your primary collection tool. From now on, if something comes your way and you are not entirely sure what needs to happen or you don't have time to go looking for the connecting information, just add it to your primary collection tool and deal with it later.

Collecting is something you are doing all the time. You want to make sure you have a way to collect with you at all times. For most, this will be a smartphone; for others, it could be something as simple as a pocket notebook carried around everywhere (Leonardo Da Vinci was a proponent of carrying pocket notes wherever you go, so it must be a good idea). Your best ideas will not come at predictable times. They are random and, in my experience, usually come at you through the three "B's" – bed, bath or bus – in other words, you are likely to be doing something unconnected to your work or projects, and an idea will strike. This is why it is important to have a means to collect the idea when it comes.

For those who prefer not to have digital devices in the bedroom, keep a notepad and pen next to your bed. When you get up the next day, you can add anything you collect to your system.

Organize

So what do you do with all this stuff you collect? Organize it. But before you can do that, you should decide what it means and what needs doing. You will find you often collect something early in the morning, and when you process what you collected, you decide you no longer want or need to deal with it, you can delete it. Never be afraid of the "delete" key. It is your best friend. The more you delete, the less you have to do, and the less gets into your system.

Organizing your collected items simply means you decide where something will go. For your tasks, you decide whether it needs to be done this week – in which case, which day this week will you do it? – Or next week, this month, next month or sometime in the future. Once you've decided, put the task in the appropriate folder in your task manager.

If you collect an idea for a project or a goal you are working on, you can add the idea to the project or goal note. You may also find you receive important information from email, Slack, or Microsoft Teams; again, you can add this information to the appropriate project note in your notes app.

> A simple way to keep your project notes clean is to avoid sending a whole email to your notes. Instead, just copy and paste the relevant information in the email to your notes. In most email apps, you can also link back to the original email if you need it.

And for any appointments you collected, you can add them to your calendar.

The important part about organizing is to keep this to the minimum amount of time possible. One area where I have seen so many mistakes is when the processing and organizing at the end of the day is longer than 30 minutes. That's too long for a daily process and organizing! You won't be consistent.

Keep in mind when you spend time processing and organizing, you are not *doing*. It often feels like you are doing something, but no work is being carried out. Nothing is being moved forward on your projects.

You will naturally be quite slow when you begin processing, as with any new skill; it takes time to learn and to become proficient. Stick with it, you will get faster, and you will refine your decision-making. The only decision you need to make about a task is *when does this need doing?*

If a project has become stuck and directionless and requires some thinking, that would be a task. You would add a task such as "review project B to see how to move to the next step." In this situation and other similar situations, that's not going to be considered *organizing* time; that would be *strategic* time. After all, sometimes we do need to step back and think about what needs to be done next on a goal or a project.

Here's a simple workflow for you to follow:

1. What is it?
2. What do I need to do?
3. When do I need to do it?
4. Where does it go?

Do

The *doing* part of COD is the key component. No amount of collecting and organizing will complete a project or achieve a goal. This is where you want to be allocating 95% of your time and resources each day. It's the doing part that gets work done, projects completed, and goals achieved.

You need a way to get ideas, commitments, and tasks into your system and to get that stuff organized; but if you are not doing the work, then all you have is a beautifully organized system and no results to show for it. What COD does is organize the basic process into easily identifiable parts so you can see where things can be improved.

For instance, when you first begin this process of getting yourself organized and have made the decision you want to be more productive, you will spend more time organizing than is optimal. That's perfectly normal. The idea is that you will develop a process that you will follow each day so that, over time, you get faster. Perhaps, at first, you spend 50 minutes cleaning up your inbox and organizing everything you have collected. If you are consistent with this and continue to find ways that refine and improve your process, those 50 minutes will fall, and you will soon be around the 25-minute mark.

Ten to twenty minutes should be the target. That's not too long, but long enough to ensure that everything is properly organized and in its right place.

There are a lot of components that fit neatly on top of this framework, such as an empowering morning routine and late-day closing-down sessions. There will be blocks of time for focused project work, and you will build in your recurring work tasks, so each day gets your most important work done. However, at the foundational level of your system will be COD.

COD ensures nothing is missed. Everything is in a place that is easily found and searchable and focuses your attention on getting the work done with the minimum amount of distraction. It's when you do not have a focus for the day, when you do not know what the plan is for the day and do not know where anything is, you could waste a lot of time just figuring out what needs doing. This can lead you to believe *everything* is important. The trouble with that is when *everything's* important, *nothing* is!

Think of COD as the skeleton of a skyscraper, critical to support the building. In normal weather conditions, the foundations and skeleton are not stressed, but normal weather conditions are not the only weather conditions we get. There are storms, hurricanes, and heavy rains. The foundations of any tall building need to be deep and strong, and the skeleton needs to support those foundations. The same applies to any good personal productivity system. The foundations need to not only support you when things are manageable; they need to support you when everything is chaotic and overwhelming.

When your days do turn chaotic (and they will), you need to know you have a system in place to collect everything so you can make decisions on these later when everything calms down. Most people rarely have problems when things are running smoothly. Problems with our workload occur when things are *not* running smoothly, and these are more common than we would like them to be.

As the African proverb says: *"calm seas do not make skillful sailors."*

As you build your personal productivity system, your first priority should be to master and optimize your collecting system. This needs to be fast and intuitive. If you have always depended on your head to remember everything, that's the first habit you will need to break and replace with a new instinctive habit to get everything that comes your way into your new system.

Your brain was not designed to remember things like that. Your brain was designed to recognize patterns. That is how we survived in the wild over many millennia. It's how we found food and water, and recognized the dangers of wild, hungry animals. It's also why we experience confirmation bias – that's where we think we can remember everything important because that's what we always do. It's why it is easy for us to point to examples of when we have remembered something, while conveniently forgetting about all the times we have forgotten something important. We look for things that confirm our current opinions.

We can use pattern recognition when we don't want to forget something in the morning. We will leave a bag or whatever we must take with us in the morning by the front door. Our brain notices that something is different from the pattern we expect and alerts us. That's why it works for us. Conversely, it can work against us, too. If you have ever been in the habit of leaving sticky notes on your computer monitor, you will notice after a while, you begin to ignore those notes. That's your brain doing what it does best. It notices a pattern, recognizes it is not a threat and will filter it out.

This means your collecting area needs to be immediately accessible on your mobile device, or your notebook must be with you everywhere you go. Ask yourself if your collecting method passes the changing trains test: if you have an idea or you remember a task you have to complete, can you get it into your system while carrying a bag and changing trains? If not, your collecting system is not good enough. Work out what you have to do to make it better.

It also means you will turn processing and organizing what you collect into a habit. If you are not clearing your inbox every 24-48 hours, it will soon fill up and become overwhelming. When that happens, you fear going in there, and that creates a negative loop. Eventually, you will stop using the system because it has become overwhelming.

Are your folders in your notes app and task manager set up correctly and easily accessible so that you can find what you need and process what you collect quickly and efficiently?

These considerations are especially important because you want to spend as much time as possible working on your goals, projects, and core work while spending as little time as possible organizing your collected stuff.

I have a rule of thumb: processing and organizing can take no more than 5% of my day. In a sense, this is more of a goal because some days I collect more than other days, and that inevitably takes more time to organize. The idea here is to avoid the trap of creating a system and allowing that system to become a place for procrastination. Intentional processing and organizing are good. Using the excuse to clean up your system when you know there is work to do is procrastination.

Become aware of how much time you spend on *managing* your tasks. Monitor it, and if you start to spend more than 10% of your day processing and organizing, ask yourself why, and take steps to refocus your energies on doing the work. The goal is to spend no more than 20 minutes each working day on processing and organizing and seek out ways to reduce that time still further.

If you process and organize every day, you will soon become faster at processing and will likely find yourself in the fifteen- to twenty-minute area. That's a good target!

In the next chapter, I am going to introduce you to a revolutionary time management system that fits perfectly with the COD system. It's a simple way to organize the tasks you collect and ensures that what you need to see today is precisely what you see.

Homework

With your new system for the next week, time yourself to see how long it takes you to process your inbox and organize the stuff you collected. The goal is to reduce this to no more than 20 minutes.

6

Setting Up The Time Sectors

*Dost thou love life? Then do not squander time, for that is
the stuff life is made of.* – Benjamin Franklin

In this chapter, I'm going to give you a simple, time-based system to organize your tasks. This is where all the things thrown at you daily, as well as the action steps you have collected for your areas of focus, are going to go.

The principle is the only thing that really matters is WHEN you will do the work. It doesn't matter what work you have to do; the only thing that matters is WHEN you will do it.

There are 24 hours in a day and 168 hours in a week. You cannot change that. You only have control over what you do in the time available to you. The Time Sector System encourages you to focus on what time you have rather than on how much work you have.

We have far more to do than time available in which to do it. Whether you are a student studying for your Ph.D. or a stay-at-home parent, there will always be more to do than time to do it in a 24-hour period. Do you go to the supermarket today or the bank or both? If you do both, you will need four hours; if you decide to do one, perhaps you will only need ninety minutes. Which is more important? When you truly understand that, and you work with time instead of against it, you find things are a lot less overwhelming and you begin to learn the art of prioritization.

The second area that the Time Sector System will help you with is focusing on the week you are in rather than worrying about anything that doesn't need doing this week. When you begin the week with a set of tasks you have decided must, or should, be done that week, you are more focused on what you are doing, and you get better at deciding what needs doing, which will lead you to get better at saying "no" to those that do not move your goals or projects forward. The other thing you will find about tasks that don't need doing this week is they have a wonderful ability to sort themselves out if you give them enough time to do so.

A trick I would encourage you to try is to default new tasks to "don't need doing this week." If you rush to get these new tasks done, you will have to find time to do them. If you slow down and move them off to next week, there will be a good chance they may no longer need doing.

This only works, though, if you commit to completing a weekly planning session each week. If you are not doing a weekly planning session, it all falls apart. The glue that brings everything together is the twenty to thirty minutes you give yourself for planning out the week ahead.

We will cover how to complete a weekly planning session later in this book, but you should learn how to proactively look at what you have to do and decide what, of all those things you have, you must do or would like to do next week. Don't worry; you get better at this over time.

No matter what productivity system you are coming from, if any, all of them have at least one element that requires you to do some planning and reviewing. These systems only work if you are *doing* the planning and reviewing. If you are not doing it, then it won't matter how beautiful or sophisticated you have things set up; it won't work in the long term.

Why focus on one week?

There are too many unknowns to worry about what may or may not happen next week. You or a family member could become sick, a project deadline may change or be canceled altogether, or some other emergency may raise its ugly head.

Because you will be doing a weekly planning session every week, you know you will have a chance to look at the following week with the information and changes you have gathered in the current week, so anything that doesn't need doing this week can be pushed off to the following week.

The Setup

Hopefully, you have a task manager to do this with; if not, and you prefer to read through this chapter to get an idea of what we are going to set up and choose your task manager later, that's fine.

THE SEVEN FOLDERS

This week

For tasks you want to complete this week

Next week

For tasks you want to complete next week

This month

For tasks you want to complete this month

Next month

For tasks you want to complete next month

Long-term / on hold

For tasks you want to at some point in the future.

Recurring Areas Of Focus

For the important tasks that come from your Areas of Focus

Routines

For those non-important must do every day/week/month tasks.

The first step is to create seven folders in your task manager. These are:

- This week
- Next week
- This month
- Next month
- Long-term and on hold
- Recurring areas of focus
- Routines

These folders are where you will store all the tasks that come into your inbox that you decide are important enough to enter your system. (Task managers generally have an inbox preinstalled. If the one you choose to use does not, then create an inbox as this is where you will collect all your tasks)

The first four folders are your "Time Sectors." This is where you put your tasks based on when they need to be done. For instance, if you have a task you decide does not need doing until next month, then you would place it into the Next Month folder. If you have a task you know needs doing over the next week or two but are not sure exactly when you will have time to do it, you place it in your This Month folder.

This Week and *Next Week* folders are obviously for tasks you want to, or need to, perform either this week or next week. How you decide will depend on two factors:

1) the urgency of the task and

2) the time you have available to perform the task.

Difficulties will arise if you treat all tasks as urgent and need doing right away. If you habitually do this, you will find you hit the fixed time problem. You cannot do everything all at once – you don't have enough time. You will need to prioritize your work and your tasks.

One of the benefits you will find with the Time Sector System is once you have decided that a task does not need to be done this week and you move the task off to next week, you will relax. You know you won't lose the task in a dark hole of hundreds of other similar tasks spread out over multiple folders. Your tasks will either need to be done this week or some other time. You know you will see tasks that do not need to be done this week when you do your next planning session.

Part of the reason we feel anxious about the amount of work we *have* to do is because we have not made a decision about *when* something will be done. This is when your brain will work against you. If you have not made a conscious decision about a task in terms of what you need to do and when you will do it, your brain will keep reminding you of it as if it were urgent – even if it is not. Your brain does not make decisions on urgency. All it does is say, "There's a task here that needs doing; I must keep reminding my human to do it." And that's what it will do. A single task like that is not much of a problem, but if you have many tasks like that, that's when you will start to feel anxious and stressed.

To eliminate that feeling, make a decision and get it into your system. You will instantly feel a lot more relaxed and less anxious.

> Have you ever noticed when you feel overwhelmed and sit down and write down everything on your mind that you think needs to be done, you feel slightly better? That's your brain letting go. If you take it to the next level and organize what you have written down by priority and when you will do it, you will feel even better.

The principle behind the Time Sector System is that there are only two things you need to know about a task:

1. What needs doing?

2. When does it need doing?

To deal with the first part, "What needs doing?" All you need to decide is what you have to do to be able to clear the task. For instance, "read through the article on implementing Agile structures in an organization" This task requires you to read through an article. It's likely to take you ten minutes. It's not urgent but does need reading before your meeting next week on Thursday.

Imagine this task doesn't have to be done this week, and you are going away for the weekend. In this scenario, this task can be dropped into the Next Week folder. No need to date anything in your next week folder because you will be doing a weekly planning session at the end of the week, and you can then decide when you will do the task.

This Month and Next Month

These folders are for tasks that do not need to be done in the immediate future but will need to be done either this month or next month. Think of your This Month folder as a place to put non-urgent tasks that you would like to complete this month.

Your Next Month is used for tasks that you want to keep around and that you would like to complete at some point in the near future. These could be tasks you may be waiting for someone else to make a final decision about, or it could be something like a reminder to take your lawn mower in for a service before Spring arrives.

Long-Term and On Hold

This folder is for all those tasks that are not due for consideration in the next three months or longer and anything that has been put on hold indefinitely, but you want to keep around for review purposes.

Anything not due in the next three months is best kept outside of your task manager and in a master task list in your notes apps. There are exceptions here. If you know for sure that a task needs to be performed on a specific date in five months' time, go ahead and add that task in there. You can add the date, and even if you rarely review your long-term and on-hold folder, it will not be missed because when the task is due, it will drop into your today list. Things like passport and residency permit renewals are examples.

What Are Routines?

In our lives, we have a lot of maintenance tasks we need to perform daily, weekly, and monthly that have no impact on our goals or projects. These are just tasks we need to complete to maintain our lives. For instance, taking the garbage out once or twice a week, washing the car, cleaning the house, doing the laundry, grocery shopping, and paying our bills.

As an adult (or even a teenager), it's unlikely you will be able to avoid many of these tasks. They just need to be done. These tasks go in the routines folder. They act as reminders and can be dated with a recurring date for when they need to be done.

Annual routine tasks can be placed here, too. It might be a bit much to put something like a passport renewal reminder in here if the passport doesn't need renewing for several years, but adding a reminder to schedule an appointment for your annual medical checkup would go in here.

Natural triggers

Some routine tasks do not need to be in your routines folder. These are tasks that have a natural trigger. For example, I previously mentioned washing your car; in reality, washing your car has a natural trigger. Every time you go to your car, you will see it is dirty and needs washing. It's likely you do not need to have a recurring task reminding you to wash it. Instead, you could simply block an hour out on your calendar for washing your car as and when you feel it needs doing. Similarly, cleaning up your computer's desktop. This is something you can see every time you work on your computer, and you could do it in between sessions of work.

Recurring Areas of Focus

This is where you put tasks and activities you have decided are part of your areas of focus. These want to be dated and set to recur as often as they need recurring.

Things like arranging a three-monthly meeting with your financial advisor, calling your parents and siblings, doing your personal development studying, and planning your next vacation would be placed inside your Recurring Areas of Focus folder.

The tasks you put in here should have a priority; after all, you have identified them as being important to you. There really is no excuse for not making sure they are appropriately prioritized. If your task manager allows you to add a flag to tasks, use that flag for these tasks.

As always, there will be exceptions. Sometimes, you will be working on a project that requires a big push to get to completion. In these cases, you may decide to prioritize the week to focus on that project. There is usually one element of the project that requires a lot of focus, and in those instances, you can block two or three days out on your calendar and focus solely on working on that project.

A quick trick if you need to block a day or two for deep, focused work on a project is to plan ahead. Trying to find a day or two next week on your calendar will likely be difficult – almost impossible. However, if you block a day or two out in a month's time, you will find the time a lot easier, and it's much easier to plan ahead and tell people you won't be available on a given day next month.

Anything inside your Recurring Areas Of Focus folder should be treated as a priority. Most people fail at achieving their goals and their life-long plans not because they lack the ability to achieve them but because they are not prioritized. Just because something needs doing right now and is screaming at you does not mean it is a priority. The words: "Thank you, I'll get that done for you later this week" are often enough to quiet the noise these tasks make.

Those are the folders you will need for the Time Sector System. You are embarking on a paradigm shift, a move away from project-based task management towards a more natural time-based system. From now on, the only decision you need to make is *when* you will do a task. That decision will be based on how urgent the task is, how important to YOU it is, and how much time you have available.

Next, we will look at where you manage your projects and how the tasks for your projects will come through into your task manager.

Homework

A great place to begin setting up your folders is to start with your routines. What do you regularly need to do just to maintain your life? For example, when do you need to take the garbage out? Clean your living room and bedroom? Put these into your task manager now and add a recurring date to the tasks. The added benefit is as you add these tasks, you will be learning how to use your task manager.

Setting Up Your Notes

Now that you know the way to set up your task manager, what we need to do next is look at how your notes app supports your task manager.

Your notes app is the home of your projects, goals and Areas of Focus statements. For this to work effectively, avoid simple text-based notes apps. You will want a notes app that allows you to throw images, links and sketches into it.

So many inputs come at us each day, making it difficult to manage them, including emails, Slack and Teams messages, instant messages, articles of interest, YouTube videos, and so much more.

The current trend in the productivity world is to find more sophisticated ways to collect and organize all this stuff. Yet, perhaps that's not the best way forward; that seems to be treating the symptom rather than going deeper to uncover the cause.

The cause is the democratization of information and the explosion of technology in the last twenty years. The internet has given us access to seemingly infinite amounts of information that just twenty years ago would have been hidden deep inside academic libraries.

I look at it like the Cambrian Explosion, where much of the life in existence today began around 530 million years ago. In evolutionary terms, it was like a loud bang, and suddenly, multiple life forms appeared. 2009 was the digital explosion. That's when, suddenly, there was an explosion in digital tools and applications that dramatically changed the workplace landscape.

Before the internet, academics used libraries to research their academic field. People interested in self-development bought books and tapes (or CDs) and attended live seminars and workshops.

An academic would spend a day or two in a library, cut off from the outside world (no mobile phones for academics working in the 1980s), where they could do uninterrupted research. (The original form of "Deep Work").

Historians would spend days, if not weeks, in the National Archives reading original papers and documents and entering their notes directly into paper notebooks.

We did not have the physical space to keep copies of all these documents and books. This meant we had to be careful about what we kept and what we left in the library.

Now, we have the convenience of the internet, which provides us with billions of documents. Everything is available to us at the press of a few buttons. Do we really need to collect all this information into our personal libraries? It's already accessible through a quick search.

If you look at the information you read, most of it will be from a passing interest. It's not always related to your vocation in life. You probably don't need to save all those web pages into your notes. The more stuff you collect, the more organizing you will have to do, reducing the time you spend doing the work that matters. Instead leave it to Google and other search engines to do the organizing for you.

If you buy things on Amazon, there is a tab at the top of the Amazon homepage called "Buy Again". You can use this tab to buy products such as your favorite tea or notebook as often as you need to

The goal is to maximize the time spent *doing* so you have more time for the things you want to do with the people or activities that mean the most to you. The goal is not to create a system that requires you to spend hours each week *maintaining*.

Apple, Google, Microsoft, and others are solving these problems for us by significantly improving their search features. I remember in 2015, I was obsessed with finding the best way to organize my digital notes. I had tags and sub-tags. I tried entrepreneur, Michael Hyatt's *Who, What, and When* method – a system based on all notes being related to a person (who), something I was interested in, or a project (what), or an event I was preparing for (when).

Ultimately, this was a lot of work. If I needed to find out how to resolve an issue with my computer, all I needed was to search Google. The answer would be there.

I used to collect all these pages that informed me how to fix something, only to discover the issue changed when Apple updated their software. It was pointless keeping documents for iOS12 when I was using iOS16, yet I did keep them because it was far too time-consuming to go through all my notes and clear out outdated ones.

A simple solution is to look at the kind of work you do. For example, let's say you attend many meetings, and keeping meeting notes is the best way to stay on top of everything. With this, all you need to do is create a note called "Meeting Notes" in your projects and place all your meeting notes in their respective project. As long as you have a clear title that contains the date the meeting was held, if you want to retrieve information from that meeting, all you would need to do is use the search feature in your notes app.

Medical professionals and lawyers must do a number of hours of continuous learning each year. Again, for this, all you would need is a folder for these learning modules. You may decide to add a few sub-folders for the different topics you study, but again, as long as you title the note well, it will be searchable in a way far faster than you could search for the document manually.

Searching for ways other people manage their notes is unlikely to help you as they do different work than you. Content creators, for instance, collect content ideas, write scripts, and plan out storylines for videos. A salesperson doesn't. A salesperson requires a way to manage their customers and prospects.

So, while you can spend a lot of time developing complex ways to structure your notes and files, if you want to build better productivity habits, perhaps spending a few seconds to ensure the titles of your notes and files contain the information you would naturally search for would be a better use of your time. It will undoubtedly result in faster results, allowing you more time to get the important work done.

Be careful before thinking you can rely on your task manager to do the information storage for you. Task managers and even more fully featured project managers are not very good at keeping little snippets of information related to a project. Information may come to you through email, Teams/Slack messages or an article may have a paragraph or two you want to keep that relates to a project (or goal) you are working on. If you try and keep this information inside a project folder in your task manager, it will be very difficult to find that information later. Task managers are not designed for storing information. Additionally, once you check off the task, the information disappears with the task. That may not be what you want. You may need to refer back to that information later. A better place for information is in the project note.

Good note apps such as Apple Notes, Microsoft OneNote, Notion, and Evernote have very powerful search features – features that will allow you to search for information based on a keyword, a title, a date, or a tag. Many of these apps will also read the text contained in an image or PDF and make that searchable. Technology is advancing so fast that you can already type the word "dog" in the search field, and you will find any image you or your partner took that includes a picture of a dog, or a mountain you climbed without the need to tag, title, or do anything else to organize it.

Notes apps can be organized by folders, which means it is easy to organize all your information into compartments related to your life. For instance:

- Goals
- Areas of Focus
- Projects
- Reference
- Archive

This makes it very easy for you to work on different compartments depending on where you are and what you are doing. For instance, if you are going away on holiday, that holiday would be classed as a project, and all your itineraries, addresses for hotels and other information can be stored there.

The Notes Folders Explained

There are numerous ways to manage your notes. The organization I have described above is simply the way I found works best for most people. I would suggest you experiment and find what works best for you. However, there are a few basic folders you can set up initially. You can change these later if you find a better way that works for you.

Goals

Having a folder where you can keep notes related to your goals and to track progress is helpful. A goal is a catalyst for change. Whether you want to reach a particular position within your company, get fit and lose weight, or be in a position to take a month off to travel through Australia, having a place in your notes where you can keep ideas, plans, and track progress is a great way to keep yourself motivated. Bigger goals may require their own folder, and in most notes apps, you can create sub-folders for these. Smaller goals may only require a single note.

You can keep your bucket list here too. Most notes apps give you the option to maintain checklists; these are great for things like bucket lists because as you check items off, they either grey out or have a line through them. This is different from how task managers work, where when you check things off, the task disappears.

Areas of Focus

This is where you keep clarifying statements for your areas of focus. While the tasks related to your areas of focus will be inside your task manager, you may want to keep your areas of focus statements in a place where you can review these periodically. I recommend you review your areas of focus every six months or so to ensure you are in balance and that you are not neglecting anything. Sometimes, we become so absorbed in a project or even an emergency that we inadvertently begin to neglect an area of focus. Reviewing your areas every three to six months as part of a weekly planning session will keep these in mind and in balance.

Your areas of focus will change over time as you go through life. Having a place where you can add notes, thoughts, and ideas will make your areas of focus folder a reassuring place to spend time. In a way, you can use this area of your notes as a journal for your thoughts over time about particular aspects of your life.

Projects

This is where you keep all your projects. Some projects may require sub-folders because of their size, while other smaller projects will only require a single note.

I don't advise you to separate work and personal projects unless you have no choice. A project is a project (just like a task is a task) and needs doing. The only difference between work and personal projects is the time you will work on those projects. While you are working on a project, you have the project folder open, so you do not see your other projects.

When you separate your work and personal life, it distorts your view of what you have to do. The days when there were hard edges between your work life and personal life have long gone. There will be times you need to talk to your daughter's school about an issue during "office hours," and equally, you may have video call early in the morning or late in the evening.

You want to be able to see everything going on in your life in one place. That way, you will be very clear about what needs to be done.

There are exceptions here. If you work for a company that strictly controls what software you have on your computers and work devices, then you will best be served by separating your personal and work notes. Another consideration would be if you left the company. Would you have time to transfer your personal projects over to a personal notes app before you leave?

One university professor I worked with had kept all her research notes in her work computer's OneNote app. When she left the university, all her research notes were deleted. There was over fifteen years 'worth of research materials lost in a matter of minutes. If you are concerned about this, I would advise you to keep your personal and professional life separate.

This is why I would strongly advise you not to use your company's built-in task managers and notes. For example, if you are using a Windows-based work computer, it's likely you will have access to Microsoft OneNote and ToDo. If you use these tools and leave the company, you are going to lose all your notes when you hand back your computer. It's safer and better to keep your notes on your personal devices. Most productivity tools allow access via a browser, so you still have access to your information when you are on your work computer; if that is not possible, you can always make sure your task manager and personal notes are kept on your phone, so you still have access to these when at work.

If you feel more comfortable keeping your work projects separate, you can use your work computer's built-in notes app for managing your work projects, but keep in mind you will need access to these when you do your weekly planning, which may be done at home.

Reference

This is where notes, web pages, and other things you want to keep for reference go. For example, my business involves online courses and coaching. I have a sub-folder dedicated to these subjects in my reference folder. I also have a folder for productivity, goal planning and time management articles I find interesting. These are all related to my work, and I may find these articles as sources of inspiration one day when I am trying to solve a client's problem or looking for a new topic for a blog post or YouTube video.

For your personal life, you may find a suppliers list that details where you can buy items of clothing, which includes your sizes for each supplier. You might also have copies of your passport, ID card and other things you may need at a moment's notice. You can also store quotes you want to keep, notes you may have taken while on a course, and ideas you may have for future vacations.

On a day-to-day basis, you will find you work more from your notes app more than any other app. When you are working on a project, you will have that project's note open, and any ideas you have, questions you may want to ask a colleague, or interesting articles that may help move the project forward can be put there.

Archive

Your archive folder is for all the notes you have finished with or for things you collected that you once had an interest in.

An archive is not a glorified trash can. It's a treasure trove of history. If you create an archive notebook or folder in your digital notes, you will be creating your own digital archive.

Because places like the National Archives in the US or UK or the archives at the Vatican City are always adding new documents, it would be impossible to organize all these documents by theme. They may be tagged by theme, but they are organized by the date they entered the archive. If I wanted to find documents related to the Titanic, I would begin my search around April 1912. If I wanted to get a snapshot of life in 1964, I would just go to the section that housed documents from 1964.

You can do the same with your own archives. Once you have created a notebook or folder called archive, you can create sub-folders or sub-notebooks by year. Then, as you archive notes, you just add them to the year they were created.

This approach will give you the all-important randomness, yet you still have some organization.

You can tag these notes if you wish; But – and this is an important but – don't try and be too clever here.

Imagine you were researching the Vietnam War and wanted to know how and why the war escalated in 1965. If you were at the US National Archives, you might begin your research in 1965, then Vietnam. So, the tag would be Vietnam. If you wanted to narrow down your research, you might look at the documents related to President Johnson's decision-making, so perhaps there would be a tag for presidential papers. Beyond that, you would be trying to fine-tune things too much. You would likely see from the results you get which documents relate to meetings.

In your archive, you may have taken a trip to Paris in 2018, and while there, you came across a fantastic restaurant. Perhaps you took at picture of the menu and saved that into your notes. Now, you have two ways of retrieving that information today. If you remember the year you were in Paris, you could go straight to your 2018 archive, and as your notes will be in date order, you could scroll down to the date you were in Paris.

The alternative is if you tagged the note "Paris," you could do a search for "Paris." And within seconds you will have retrieved the information you wanted.

That's how you want your notes to work. Keep them simple, so that if you want to retrieve information later, you would be able to find things quickly.

What I've noticed is when we are too strict about how we organize our notes we are always fiddling and changing things. While this can be fun, at first, it becomes a drag on your productivity.

You could create separate notebooks for places and topics, but unless these are lifetime interests, keeping everything in their separate notebooks will not make retrieval any faster, and you lose that all-important randomness.

Another area where randomness really helps is with your ideas and thoughts. I'm sure you've had an idea about classes you may want to take or a business idea you want to investigate. You may have had ideas about starting a blog or podcast or writing a book. Many of these ideas will be passing ideas and you soon move on to the next idea. If you were intent on doing something about the idea, you would begin. If you don't begin, it's probably a passing idea.

These passing ideas are the gold you do not want to delete. They could contain the seeds of something very special. On their own, they may seem redundant after a few weeks or months. It's these notes you want to keep in your archive.

In a year or two, you may feel compelled to skim through one of your archive years, and you begin to see connections between all these ideas. Leonardo Da Vinci sketched the mouth he eventually gave the Mona Lisa twelve years before he began painting the Mona Lisa.

Individually, these notes may mean nothing. But together, they could be your next great idea.

When do you transfer tasks to your task manager?

If you are in a project meeting, give yourself a couple of minutes after the meeting to transfer any tasks that need doing to your task manager's inbox. These could be things like "send Patricia a copy of the project outline" or "update the project status in the Excel file." These tasks have a timeline. It could be you promised to send Patricia the project outline later today/tomorrow, or the project leader asked you to update the Excel file. If you left a task like this in your project note, you are not going to see it until you next work on that project, which could be days later.

Tasks like "test out changing the header to blue" likely don't have a specific time and can be handled next time you work on the project. For something like this, you don't need to send it to your task manager.

From now on, manage your projects from your notes app. It's a much more intuitive way to manage projects.

If I haven't convinced you yet that your notes app is the best place to manage projects, then the killer advantage of using a notes app is when you cross out a task in a notes app, the task does not disappear. It just has a line through it. This way, if you are asked if something has been done, you have a record. You can add a date when you completed it if that makes you feel more comfortable.

In a task manager, once a task has been completed, it disappears from the list. In many task managers, you can go hunting for it once it has been completed. But that adds another step to something that can be easily achieved in your notes app.

The Entrepreneurial Mind

Are you one of those people whose mind never stops coming up with great ideas? If you are, then you have what I term the "entrepreneurial mind." This is the kind of mind that will wake you up at 2:30 am with a brilliant idea, and you become anxious if you do not collect it somewhere.

The problem is not that you have a lot of great ideas (that is generally a good thing); the problem is collecting and referencing those ideas later. Unfortunately, you will soon discover that time is working against you. To develop and work on all these great ideas would require more time than you have available. If you are someone who generates a lot of ideas, you can create a note in your reference area and call it something like "Ideas vault." You can then collect all these ideas together, and if you do find yourself with free time or you remember you had an idea that could work with a project you are working on, you can find the idea and develop it.

A quick tip here is to keep these ideas in a single note. Your brain has an amazing ability to connect ideas together. Something you collected last July may become relevant again when you see an idea you collected in February. Your brain makes a connection and suddenly a good idea has become a great idea. When you go through your ideas, you will easily see any connections. If you keep all your ideas in separate notes, it will be much harder to make those connections.

With this kind of note, I would also suggest you create a recurring task in your task manager, reminding you to review it periodically. Just for reference, I review my ideas note every three months at the end of the quarter.

The Anchor Note

The anchor note is a single note with information you regularly need to access. For instance, in Korea, if you order something from abroad, you need a Personal Customs Number. This is a ten-digit number that is not easy to remember. I have this number in my Anchor Notes note, which means it is easy to access from any device I am on. I also keep links to websites I regularly reference or share with other people. For example, I use a scheduling service that allows people to schedule appointments with me without having to go back and forth trying to figure out time zone differences. My scheduling service provides me with a link I can share with other people, and they can then pick a time most suitable for them. That link is in my Anchor Notes, where it is easily accessible.

Most notes apps will allow you to pin this note to the top of your notes list so it's quick and easy to access whenever you need it.

Now, let's look at where your calendar comes into this mix.

Setting Up Your Calendar

The third and final part of your tool kit is your calendar. You need little to do to set this up except create two calendars: one for work and one for personal use. You can then give each a different color.

When you have different colors denoting what your events are for, it helps you gain a better view of where you are spending your time. Too much work color, and you will instantly see that in your calendar. We are looking for a balance between your employed work and your personal life.

In the chapter on your goals and areas of focus , I mentioned that if one of your areas of focus was to be fit and healthy, you can schedule this on your calendar. When will you do your exercise, and how frequently? This would be something you put on your calendar, not on your task list.

> If exercise and keeping fit is a big part of your life, you may wish to consider creating an exercise calendar with its own unique color. This way, at a glance, you can see how consistent you have been with your exercise.

> Similarly, it can be useful to have a calendar set up with your family as a shared calendar. That way, your family members can see when there are any family events such as birthday parties, weddings, sports events involving kids, etc. I also have a separate calendar for my meetings and calls. This way, I can see how many meetings I have in the week when I am planning the week.

The way to look at this is if something needs a given amount of time and must be done at a specific time, then it goes on your calendar. For example, a meeting at 2 pm would be on your calendar, not on your task list. The same applies to exercise. It needs time, and unless you commit to a time, you are probably going to find exercise will be one of those sacrificial tasks that will be ignored when you feel busy or if a last-minute request comes in from a colleague or boss.

To get you started, go through your goals and areas of focus and find the things that require you to spend time doing each week. For instance, if you decided to study French, how much time would you study? When will you study? In the morning, between 6:30 am and 7:30 am? Or would you prefer to study in the evening?

Your calendar will never lie to you. You only have twenty-four hours each day to fit in everything you need to do. Your higher-level goals will not be accomplished on their own – you have to find time to do the action steps required consistently. Your calendar shows you precisely how much time you have available each day beyond your commitments. A financial goal may only require you to send an amount of money to your savings account each month; that would be on your task list – you can do that at any time of the day. But if one of your goals is to achieve a master's degree, you will need considerable time to study. Your study time needs to be on your calendar.

Writers such as John Grisham block out time for writing. At 7:30 am, armed with a cup of coffee, Grisham will begin writing. He will write for around four hours, and that's it. In his writing office, there is no phone or internet. It's just four hours of writing. He does that five days each week. Ian Fleming, author of the James Bond books, also wrote in the morning. From 9:00 am to 12:00 pm, he would go into his living room and write. Again, there were no distractions. Ian Fleming wrote, on average, 2,000 words per day. Do that five days a week; you have 10,000 words a week. Over eight weeks, you have a book.

Ian Fleming wrote at his Jamaican bungalow between December and March each year between 1952 and 1964. Today, you can visit that bungalow, as the property has been developed into a resort hotel. If you ever need inspiration to live a focused, productive life, that might be something you may want to put on your bucket list. The name of the resort? Goldeneye!

Consider that both these accomplished writers wrote consistently for three to four hours a day and still had time for other things. They knew what their core work was and made sure they had the time to do it.

To give you an example from my own life, my work week requires me to write one blog post, two newsletters and a podcast script each week. I also need time to plan out and record my YouTube videos as well as the podcast. This is part of my core work each week. The only way I can consistently get these done each week is to fix the time required to do them on my calendar.

How Author Jeffrey Archer Structures His Day

To help you see the power of getting control of your calendar, here's how author Jeffrey Archer structures his day by using the power of his calendar.

Jeffrey Archer has a unique writing process that involves eight hours of writing each day and six hours for rest. He begins his writing day at 6:00 am, where he will write for two hours. At 8:00 am, he takes a break for two hours and returns to writing at 10:00 am. He will then do a further two-hour writing session and, at 12:00 pm, take another two-hour break. He will continue this two-hour work, two hours rest routine through the day until 8:00 pm when he stops for the day.

What's remarkable about this routine is its length. Authors such as John Grisham will write for four hours a day and then stop. Archer writes for eight hours. That's a long day.

Know Your Core Work

Authors, in general, and Archer, in particular, know their core work: writing. Each day is focused on writing, and while they are writing, nothing is allowed to interrupt or distract them.

Jeffrey Archer still has obligations to his publisher, editors, and readers, yet he knows he would not get any writing done if he spent all day answering their questions and queries.

What is your core work? What are you employed to do? How much time do you spend on your core work each day? No matter what you are hired to do, something is at the core of your work. As you saw in the chapter on core work, whether you are a truck driver, a teacher, or a doctor, you have a set of core work activities you prioritize over everything else. Your day will be more productive if you build it around doing your core work activities.

Allow Time For Other Things

If you look at Archer's day, he has six hours of non-writing time. During that time, he eats and exercises, but he also has time for dealing with communications, meetings, exercise, administrative tasks, and any other business he may need to take care of.

If you have four to six hours each day to deal with other people's questions and requests, would that be enough time? I would guess for most people the answer would be yes. If that is the case, would it be possible to block two hours each day for completely focused work on your core work?

Jeffrey Archer has a very active social life; it's entirely possible in his daily schedule to have lunch with a friend and do his daily walk during his 12 until 2 p.m. break. His 4 p.m. to 6 p.m. break could be dedicated to dealing with his communications for the day. In his schedule, there is more than enough time to complete his non-core work, and he still spends eight hours doing core work. (Although you may not want to work a fourteen-hour day).

Be Disciplined

The many years I've spent studying successful people has shown me the key ingredient to their success is self-discipline.

In a talk Archer gave to the Oxford University Union, he spoke of some mornings waking up and thinking, "Do I have to go through this again?" yet he would still pull himself out of bed and head to his office. He knows once he writes the first sentence, the hardest part of the day is done.

In the same talk, Archer said he has not had to work since publishing his third book, *Kane And Abel*, in 1979. The success of that book made him a multi-millionaire, yet he still gets out of bed at 5:30 AM every day.

Do you ever not do something because you simply don't feel like doing it, even though you know it needs to be done or else there will be consequences? What's stopping you is not the work; it's taking the first step. This is why if you want to write a book or start a podcast, the best thing you can do is start writing or recording. Once you've done that, you're committed.

The hardest part is the first step or sentence. Focus on doing that one thing, and the rest will follow.

Love The Process

As we looked at when I suggested you reframe the way you look at your work – changing it from a job to a way to grow your knowledge and education – all authors I have learned about fall in love with the process of writing. Almost all of them follow the same or similar routine daily. That predictability makes it easy for them to overcome distractions and feelings of not being in the mood and get the work done consistently.

The best salespeople I have ever worked with were equally as disciplined when it came to prospecting and finding new customers. Those of us who were less good, we gossiped over coffee and waited for customers to come through the door. It doesn't take a genius to figure out why I was not a great salesperson.

When Archer sits down to write the first sentence of a new book, he is twelve drafts and nine months away from a finished book. If he were focused on the result, it would be demoralizing and even painful. Instead, he knows if he follows a process each day for the next nine months, the book will, in effect, write itself.

It's the process that will get you through difficult days and give you the results you want. If you wish to write a book, learn a new language, or achieve your Ph.D., you will not get there on the first day. You won't get there in the first week or month. It takes time and a process. Find your process and fall in love with it.

No matter what you do, there's something you can learn from the writing success of Jeffrey Archer. He's in his mid-eighties, no longer needs to earn money, and has a happy family life, yet he still gets up in the morning and writes. Like all of us, he has days when he doesn't feel in the mood, yet he will still go to the office and write. He knows his core work and makes sure he spends time on that core work each day. It's that focus on the core work that delivers a book each year.

And that little story takes us nicely into the next section: *time blocking*.

What is Time Blocking?

Time blocking is simply allocating blocks of time to do specific types of work. This does not mean you block time out to write an individual email; if you do have an email to write, you block out time on your calendar for "Communications," where you can deal with all your emails in one block. Likewise, if you have an important project to complete and know you will require around three hours, block that time out on your calendar. You only need to select a three-hour block (or two ninety-minute blocks) and call it "Project work."

Your task manager or project note will tell you what needs to be worked on. Your calendar tells you when you have the time to do it.

For example, I have four blocks of time for "writing" each week on my calendar. I also have an "Audio/Visual time" block for recording my videos and podcasts. Knowing I have these blocks fixed into my calendar each week means I never have to worry about completing my work. It gets done because each week, I have time scheduled for it. If it does not get done, I only have myself to blame for not protecting my time.

> In January 1952, Ian Fleming walked into the living room of his bungalow in Jamaica at 9:00 am. He closed the shutters on the windows, sat down at his typewriter, and began typing. He typed until noon, put the typed sheets into his desk drawer, and went for his lunch. Ian Fleming repeated that process every day for six weeks. At the end of those six weeks, he had in his briefcase the first draft of a story that would be the "spy story to end all spy stories."

Those six weeks in 1952 birthed the most famous spy in modern times. The book was called *Casino Royale*, and it introduced the world to James Bond.

How did Ian Fleming do that? He did it by blocking time out each morning to sit down and write. He made sure everyone in his household, from his wife to guests staying with him in Jamaica, knew he was not to be disturbed during those times. It was such a successful formula that he repeated the same routine every year when he was in Jamaica for the next twelve years until his death in 1964.

You need to set aside time for whatever you want to do. We cannot change the time we have each day, but we can choose and change our activities.

To make this work, once an event is scheduled on your calendar, it happens. Of all your tools – task manager, notes app, and calendar – the rule to adopt is: *"what goes on my calendar gets done."* You require one non-negotiable place. However, this does not mean you cannot be flexible. If a last-minute urgent meeting that cannot be rescheduled is called at a time you have blocked for something else, you can always reschedule your previous event. The important thing is you do not ignore what you have committed to. Reschedule, by all means; just don't ignore.

Elon Musk, founder of Tesla and other companies is alleged to segment his day into five minute blocks. Each block is allocated something. That is not time blocking; that is micro-managing, and you want to avoid doing this. It would be impossible to micromanage every minute of the day. Meetings overrun; you get pulled up in the hall for a chat with a colleague, or a customer will call you with an urgent request.

Maya Angelou, the author and Civil Rights activist would go to a hotel each day at 7 am to write, think and plan. She would finish at 2 pm and after that would walk home, shop and cook dinner or meet with friends. The hard work had been done – the seven hours of writing and thinking – the rest of the day was flexible. This is why the goal is to eliminate, not accumulate. Be the gatekeeper of your calendar.

Time blocking means you block out time for the essential things that need to be done – the non-negotiables. For example, when will you study if you are preparing for an exam? If you decide to study for ten hours preparing for that exam this week, you would block out, say, two hours in the evening for five days. It does not mean you block out the whole evening with time for dinner, showering, and watching a little TV. The only block you require is for your study time. You can fit your dinner, shower, and TV watching around your study time.

In the 1990s, when Michael Dell (of Dell Computers) had a young family, he would always be home by 6 pm for the family dinner. He would then spend time with his wife and kids, and when the kids went to bed, he would go into his home office and clean up the day for an hour. That time was flexible, but it allowed him precious time for his family, and he was still able to do a little work before retiring for the day.

Renegotiating Your Commitments

You can set a time each day when you can adjust your appointments and events on your calendar, and that is when you complete your daily planning session. We will cover the two important planning sessions later in the book, but for now, when you do an end-of-day planning session, you look at your appointments for the next day, and if you see a conflict or you realize you may be being a little too ambitious with your commitments, you can move things around.

> When you begin using the Time Sector System, you will most likely be over-ambitious. There will be a strong urge to load up your daily task list and block out a lot of time for activities. This is the learning process. It is human nature to overestimate what we can accomplish in a day. It's at this point that many people blame or beat themselves up. Don't do that! You're human. If you do find yourself not completing your tasks or missing some time blocks, ask yourself why you were unable to do them. The chances are it's simply because you were being a little overambitious.

> Bill Gates remarked: "Most people overestimate what they can do in one year and underestimate what they can do in ten years."

> You can apply that to your day as well. Most people overestimate what they can do in a day and underestimate what they can do in a week.

> When using your calendar, look at what you want to accomplish in the week rather than what you feel you must do each day. This will take a lot of pressure off your day, and if you do have a slow day or an unforeseen emergency arises, you can deal with that and renegotiate your commitments for the rest of the week.

Now, you need to apply a little mindset trick. Once you have planned out your day and committed to all the events on your calendar, they are now fixed unless an absolute emergency happens. Make them non-negotiable. No one is allowed to break that commitment with you. When you begin to trust yourself with this, you will find not only does your productivity improve, but so does your sleep. Part of the reason we feel anxious and stressed about our work is because we sense we do not have time to complete everything we have committed to. One of the powerful features of the Time Sector System is you very quickly learn what you can accomplish each day and each week, and that helps you plan out your week and leaves you knowing that you have enough time to complete the work you plan to do.

So now you have your task manager, your notes app and your calendar set up. You are ready to move to the next stage, which is to bring in the mechanics of how the Time Sector System works for you on a day-to-day basis. Before we do so, let's recap what each of your digital tools are for:

Your Task Manager

This is where your tasks will go. You use your task manager to decide which tasks you need to complete and which ones you need to work on this week. This is broken down into individual days. Your task manager takes care of the micro-level activities of your day.

You are unlikely to complete all your assigned tasks each day, and that is fine. From now on, you want to see things as "these are the tasks I want to complete this week." If you don't complete all your Monday tasks, you can move the remaining tasks off to another day that week.

Your Notes App

This is where you will manage your goals, areas of focus, and projects. Each goal, area, and project will, at the very least, have its own note. If the goal or project is large, you can create a sub-folder to keep all the various materials you need.

Inside your notes, you will store images, screenshots, pasted snippets of information, and important emails related to the project. When you are working on a project, you will have the project note open, and you can work from there. Your task manager just tells you, "Continue work on project X." You then will come to your project note and begin work.

Your Calendar

This is the tool that ensures whatever you put in it gets done. No excuses! If you have scheduled a two-hour Spanish language study session at 6 pm and you come home tired; no excuses. Get your books out and study. Remember: *What goes on your calendar gets done*. (Although what is important here is not the time; it's that you *do* the studying. If you can only manage one hour, that's great. You did some studying).

Your calendar reassures you that you have the time to get the important things in your life completed.

Homework

If you have not done so already, get yourself set up with some tools. Remember, you can choose the built-in tools on your digital devices for now. The important thing is you have a set of tools to begin with.

7

What Are You Employed To Do?

"Take my advice: take everything you've received today and put it away; don't touch it for a week. Urgent, not urgent-leave it, don't touch it. Come back to it after seven days, ten days. This is what you'll see – ninety per cent will take care of itself, and the ten per cent that didn't – that's probably what you need to deal with." – Yitzhak Shamir (Former Israel Prime Minister)

Your Core Work

In this chapter, you will learn how to prioritize the work that matters: the work you are employed to do and the key to excelling at the work you are evaluated on. This work directly gives you the results you seek whether you are a landscape gardener or a self-employed accountant.

In the next section, you will learn how to set up your task manager and integrate your notes. However, before we get there, we need to look at how to prevent your task manager from becoming your master. Your task manager is there to serve you, to be a place to offload everything you want to remember so you minimize the chance of missing something important. It needs to be your servant, never your master.

What is a task manager? A task manager could be a paper notebook where you collect the things you need to do (tasks). Each day, you would select a number of those tasks as the tasks you will complete today.

These days, there are some excellent task management applications you can have on your phone, tablet, and computer. These applications will do a lot of the organizing for you. We will go into more detail on how to use these in the next chapter; however, for now, we need to know what we want to put into this task manager.

The challenge we face when we become adept at collecting stuff is we collect unimportant tasks, too. This is perfectly normal, but when this happens, important tasks can become swamped by low-value tasks – tasks that, if left alone, would take care of themselves. However, at the point of collection, we are unlikely to know the value of what we have until we process them later.

So, how do you keep the important tasks from getting lost in an ocean of low-value tasks? This is easier than you may think; all it takes is a little forward-thinking.

Let's begin with a question: *What are you employed to do?*

If you are employed as a salesperson, you are hired to sell your company's products or services. Your income will likely be determined by how much you sell, whether you are paid a commission or a bonus for exceeding your targets (or both).

Any activity that directly or indirectly leads to a sale would be important. Therefore, any activity that puts you at risk of making a sale would be considered a core work task.

Medical doctors have the Hippocratic Oath, which is a set of ethics doctors swear to uphold. One of the clauses states:

"I will apply, for the benefit of the sick, all measures that are required, avoiding those twin traps of overtreatment and therapeutic nihilism."

And there, you have a sentence that encapsulates the essence of a doctor's core work.

Your core work is any activity that gives you the results you are employed to achieve. For instance, a teacher is employed to teach, a doctor is employed to treat sick patients, and a truck driver is employed to drive a truck. Whatever your position, there will likely be a clue to your core work in your job title.

A manager manages people, departments, or products; a coach coaches people to become better at something, and a software developer develops software.

The best way to understand your core work is to look at your responsibilities, and you are likely to find that either in your job title, job description or annual evaluation report. Either of these will give you a clear understanding of what your company expects of you.

Once you have found your key responsibilities, ask yourself what you need to do to discharge those responsibilities satisfactorily. For example, if you were hired as a podcast producer, what do you need to do to create that podcast each week? These tasks could be:

- Invite guests.
- Research the guests.
- Prepare questions.
- Record the podcast.
- Edit the podcast.
- Publish the podcast.
- Promote the podcast on social media.

That's seven tasks. As a podcast producer, these tasks would be your core work. If you were to skip any of these tasks, you would not be doing your job, you would miss deadlines, and you would not be delivering the results you were hired to deliver.

Your boss may want you to download the listening figures each month, but as a podcast producer would that be a core work task? Possibly not. If not, you would never prioritize that task over the seven core work tasks you have in this example.

What about a pharmaceutical salesperson? What would their core work look like? Pharmaceutical salespeople have a unique challenge. In most countries, they are not permitted to sell directly to the end user (the patient), and in countries with government-provided healthcare, they cannot sell directly to the body that purchases the drugs (the government). Instead, they can only sell to doctors who are authorized to prescribe the drug (the decision makers).

The goal here is to develop relationships with the doctors who prescribe the drugs and sell the benefits of their product over the competition. This can only be achieved by being in contact with the doctors who make the decisions on what to prescribe – commonly called "Key Opinion Leaders."

A pharmaceutical salesperson's core work in this situation is, therefore, going to be centered around communication. Here, the best form of communication is face-to-face, followed by telephone/video calls and email. This means the core work for such a person could be:

- Call X number of doctors to arrange appointments.
- Collect the latest information on authorized clinical trial data.
- Email authorized research data to Key Opinion Leaders.
- Attend appointments.

If you are a salesperson, your core work is not filling out activity reports for your sales manager, attending weekly in-house sales meetings or completing your expense report. While these tasks may need to be addressed, they should never be prioritized over any core work task.

Similarly, a truck driver's core work is picking up the goods to be delivered and driving those goods to their destination. At a task level, that would involve knowing where the pickup point is and what the goods are (to ensure the right trailer is attached to the truck), confirming the right drop-off point, and having the correct paperwork. Their core work is not completing government environmental/activity reports or fuel data sheets. Again, while these tasks need to be done, they should not be prioritized over the core work.

One of the advantages of clearly understanding what your core work is (and is not) is that you create a natural system for prioritizing your work. With practice, you instinctively know what to prioritize, making deciding what should be done each day almost automatically.

If you've ever had the misfortune of attending a hospital's emergency room, you may have noticed a process being played out. This process has a name: Triage. Triage means from the moment you arrive in the emergency room, a key medical professional will assess you on a scale of one to five, with each one being given a color.

These are:

- **Level 1.** A red patient needs immediate critical care as their life is in imminent danger.
- **Level 2.** A yellow patient needs immediate attention, although their life is not in immediate danger.
- **Level 3.** Green patients do not have a life-threatening injury and can be seen in order of appearance.

- **Level 4.** The patient is either already deceased or has sustained a life-ending injury. There is nothing the medical professionals can do to save this patient.

- **Level 5.** The patient has no injury or does not need any medical assistance.

Different medical institutions may employ variations on this triage, but the purpose is the same: to be able to quickly identify which patients need attention and which ones can wait. This process was devised for military medical personnel who are often called to incidents where there are multiple injuries, and there is a need to quickly assess which patients need immediate attention, who can wait and who are beyond help. (You really do not want to be in the beyond help category).

Establishing your core work is very similar to triage. Multiple tasks are coming at you throughout the day, and you need a process where you can quickly assess the importance of each task and make a decision about when (or if) you will do the task. For example, if you were a screenwriter, your core work would be writing scripts. Deadlines are tight, and producers and directors request scene rewrites daily. If you were receiving emails and messages about your availability to write more scripts, these messages would not be your core work. They are important but not your core work. Responding to these messages could be done between your writing sessions, or you may dedicate an hour at the end of the day to deal with these and other messages that may have come in.

You could also take inspiration from medical triage and assign different levels to your core work. The critical work that you must do could be assigned Level 1 and the least important tasks could be assigned Level 5.

To keep your core work front and center of your day, the tasks that trigger you to do the necessary work can be placed in your task manager.

An example here would be a teacher. Part of a teacher's core work would be preparing for her classes. If our teacher decided they needed one hour to organize their materials, the tasks associated with this preparation would come up each time they needed to do their class preparation. A task would look like this:

Print out lesson materials for students.

Similarly, if you were the CEO of a company and had documents and a presentation to prepare for a monthly board meeting, the tasks associated with the preparation would be in your task manager and set to repeat when you needed to begin the preparation. A task for this might look like:

Work on the presentation for next week's board meeting.

Make Use of Your Calendar

Because our teacher knows they need an hour each day to prepare their lessons, they would block out time when they could prepare their class materials. A teacher can likely fix this time each day, although that will depend on their teaching schedule.

If our CEO knows they need to begin their preparation a week before the board meeting, they could block an afternoon out each month to work on their preparation. So, for example, if the board meeting is every month on the last Thursday, the CEO could block the afternoon a week before that date every month to prepare for the board meeting.

Your calendar is a critical tool for your core work because this is the work that must be done – it is what you are employed to do. Using your calendar is the best way to ensure you have the time to do this critical work.

One error I see people making here is resisting blocking time out to do this core work. The thinking is they need a lot of flexibility for urgent meetings and dealing with crises. The trouble here is if you do not do these important, core work tasks, then when will you do them? If you are not scheduling time to do these tasks, you will run out of time during your regular working hours, and that means either you work late or spend part of your weekend catching up. Neither is a good option.

Look at it this way: a doctor is not going to leave a level 1 patient lying on a trolley because their ward manager wants them to answer an administrative question. Similarly, an airline pilot is not going to skip their pre-flight checks because someone at the head office requires a copy of a flight plan from last week. Core work comes first, *then* everything else.

Leaders and Core Work

Being a leader in an organization brings unique challenges when establishing core work. It's not always clear what the core is from a job title: Chief Executive Officer, Vice-President of Product Development, or Finance Director does not immediately elicit a clear idea of what the role involves. However, when faced with unclear core work tasks, an excellent place to go is how the individual leadership role is defined.

I have studied many successful leaders over the years, and one thing that has stood out for me is how these leaders define their roles. An excellent example of great leadership is Christian Horner at Red Bull Racing. Christian Horner is not only the team principal of the Formula 1 racing team but also the CEO of the Red Bull Powertrains company.

In interviews about his leadership style, he often talks about seeing his role as removing obstacles and friction points so his team can get on and do their job. He also talks about his job being about communicating team goals with clarity and being approachable. These ideas on the role of a leader are also echoed by other successful team principles in Formula 1. For example, Guenther Steiner, formerly at HAS Racing, and Toto Wolff at Mercedes Benz talk a lot about barrier removal and fostering a team culture where staff can tell their leaders where they think they are wrong.

These elements of a leader's role are good places to start if you are in a leadership position. You can begin by asking yourself a few questions:

- Do I communicate regularly with my team?
- Does my team clearly understand the goals of our department/company?
- Am I clearing the way so there are no obstacles to my team doing their work to the best of their abilities?

You can build your core work tasks from the answers to these questions. For example, scheduling regular meetings with your key team members, ensuring you do a daily walk around your department to find out if there is anything your team needs that will help them do their work faster and better, and reminding your team of the goals you have set for your area of responsibility.

Great leaders serve their teams and people. What can you do that will serve your team in a way that enhances their abilities to do their job?

> "Well, of course, you'll have to read all the briefs, and we'll rush you from place to place, shaking hands with people. But other than that, well, there are lots of things people want you to do and lots of things you should do, and any number of things you can do, but very few things you have to do. It's up to you; you're the boss." – Bernard Woolley, Prime Minister's Principle Private Secretary, in the BBC political sitcom *Yes, Prime Minister*.

I once spoke with a Vice President of Operations at an engineering company who told me, "I am in overall charge of plant management, which consists of the safety of factory personnel, plant productivity and plant maintenance. In addition, I am responsible for meeting production targets and the annual budget."

This is a crystal clear definition of this vice president's core work. If this were you, all you need to do now is to identify what that looks like at a task level.

Take the safety of the factory personnel; what would that look like at a task level? Perhaps you could make it your first task of the day by looking through the accident report book. This would inform you what factory accidents occurred over the last 24 hours. You can then decide whether safety protocols need attention or not.

Next would be to look at how many units were completed the previous day. This can then be measured against your targets. Any issues can then be raised with the relevant people.

Once you have defined your core work, it can be relatively easy to develop tasks that ensure you are paying attention to those things for which you are responsible.

Business Owners And Core Work

Identifying the core work of business owners can be challenging because when you start a business, the chances are you will be doing everything: sales, operations, Human Resources, finance, website design, communications, customer support and many other things. With so many roles, it can take a lot of work to identify not only your core work but also how to fit all those tasks into a week.

The key here is to start with how to serve your customers best. When running a business, the worst thing you can do is to get lost in the minor administrative tasks while neglecting your existing and potential customers. Talking directly with a potential customer is always more important than designing your company's logo.

Begin with how you can best serve your customers. This means more than just your existing customers but your potential customers. For instance, if you provide bookkeeping services for small to medium-sized companies in your local area, your core work would focus on ensuring your clients' accounts are up to date and marketing your services to potential clients. This means defining what, at a task level, you need to do each day to maintain the accounts of your existing clients and deciding how much time each day (or week) you will spend on marketing your services.

Let's say you decide writing a blog post each week about small business finances is something you must do as part of your marketing. When will you write your weekly blog post? Writing this week's blog post becomes the task, and you may need to block an hour on your calendar each week for this. You could dedicate three hours in the morning and two hours in the afternoon to working on your clients' books. While you may not need to create individual tasks for each client, you would still block time on your calendar for working on the accounts.

Whether you are employed or run your own business, identifying your core work and distilling that down to the task level ensures you can quickly identify what is important and what is not. Once you have the tasks, you can enter them into your task manager and set them to recur as frequently as needed.

You could also block the time out on your calendar for the bigger tasks – tasks that need an hour or more to complete. For example, a part of my core work is to write a blog post, two newsletters and a podcast script each week. I know I need around six hours each week to complete these tasks. On my calendar, I have a two-hour writing time block between 9:30 am and 11:30 am on both Monday and Tuesday. I also have a "floating" two-hour time block on a Thursday, which allows me the option to move the block around if necessary. Because Monday's and Tuesday's blocks are fixed, I know never to arrange meetings or anything else at that time. That time is reserved for my writing. This means I already know I have enough time to do my core work before the week starts. All I have to do is be disciplined enough to respect time and protect it from time thieves.

Now, this throws up an interesting dilemma. Imagine you had a family emergency that took up a large part of the week. This meant you were unable to write your weekly blog post – something you have identified as being a critical part of your marketing plan and, therefore, a core work task. You also have a lunch appointment with a former colleague scheduled for Friday that will involve an hour's drive there and back and perhaps ninety minutes for lunch. In total, three and a half hours.

An objective solution here would be to reschedule the lunch. After all, you have a valid reason: there was a family emergency. Chatting with your former colleague is not likely to result in a sale, but writing the blog post potentially could. This means while it would be very nice to catch up with your ex-colleague, it's not a part of your core work and, therefore, should not take priority over your core work task.

A client of mine runs his own business. The business provides IT services to local companies, and there are around 35 employees. Once my client learned about the power of identifying core work, he rolled it out to the rest of his company. Each individual has a set of clear core work task objectives each week. They are empowered to block time out each week on their calendars to make sure they have sufficient time to carry out their core work, and management is expected to respect that time.

The great thing about ensuring your team has sufficient time to carry out their core work tasks is that you now have a simple way to measure where processes or the work an employee does need adjusting or changing. Your employees are clear from the start of each week about what needs to be done, and they can arrange their work week around getting these tasks done.

Where could you block time on your calendar for doing your core work?

We will look at managing your calendar in a later chapter.

Homework

Over the next week, monitor the tasks you do at work. Which of those tasks would you consider critical to your work, and what tasks were not? To help you, consider any task delegated to you by your boss or colleague as not being core work. Additional tasks may need doing, as in the example of truck drivers filling out environmental impact and fuel data reports, but they are not your core work.

8

Why Set Goals?

Your goals are little flurries of intense activities that drag you kicking and screaming back on track.

In the previous chapters, we looked at your areas of focus and your core work, and I alluded to where your goals fit in. Goals are often explained as big, hairy and scary things that only a few lucky people can achieve. This is not true. A goal can be anything you make it. You could make it a goal to go to bed at 11:00 pm tonight or to wake up at 6:00 am. These are both goals.

The best way to look at a goal is as a mechanism to pull you back on course with your areas of focus. Goals are not the final destination, that is reserved for your areas of focus – becoming the person you want to become. If you consider it for a moment, many high schoolers have the goal of getting into a top university. For those that achieve that goal, is that the end? No, not at all. Getting into university is just a step along a career path.

Goals can be short-term, such as losing a little weight, or a longer-term goal, to become a consultant surgeon at a major hospital. But what you will find is the goals you stick with are the ones that are connected in some way to your areas of focus.

For example, you may want to build your own business, which would be connected to your career/business area of focus. If you have begun the process of starting your business but, for one reason or another, you have not done anything about it for a few months, you could create a goal to restart and complete one of the tasks.

Imagine you wanted to design and sell notebooks for students, but you stopped at ordering the samples from a Japanese paper manufacturer. You may set the goal of getting the samples ordered and delivered to you in 90 days' time.

Setting a goal gives you a focal point; it moves you from where you are today to where you want to be in the future. However, for you to successfully accomplish your goal, there needs to be some parameters as well as some "rules of engagement."

With the student notebooks, I could set the parameters as completing the design within 14 days and finalizing who to request samples from by the end of the first month. The rules of engagement will be to continue designing the notebook for an hour each day and to spend thirty minutes researching Japanese paper companies.

If you look at the breakdown here, I have a "what" – to get the samples of my student notebooks. I automatically have a "why" because where I currently am with my business plans is not where I desire to be, and I have a "how" – to work on my designs and research manufacturers.

The structure of an effective goal is *what*, *why*, and *how*. What do you want, why do you want it, and how are you going to get it? Of these three, the most difficult one is the why. Why do you want to achieve this goal? The *why* is also the most important part of achieving your goal. Why is the motivation that will keep you going when things become challenging (and they will if the goal is worthwhile)

The good news is if you have spent time developing your areas of focus, you will already have your why. Your why is the definition you gave to each of the eight areas of focus.

The "why" needs to be genuinely personal and not covertly personal. By that, I mean your *why* needs to be for *you* and not for other people. For example, losing weight to impress other people rarely works. However, losing weight to get healthy so you can enjoy a long and healthy life often does work. The goal's motives are working at a higher purpose.

The Problem With SMART Goals

For years, the advice has been that if you want to set a goal, your goal needs to be SMART: *Specific, Measured, Achievable, Realistic,* and *Timed*.

Now, broken down in this way, you would think if you were clear about what you would like to achieve, it's realistic, and you have a way to measure your progress over a given period, hitting your goals would be easy. Well, yes and no.

Setting SMART goals can and does work inside a company, and the reason for that is why SMART goals don't work for individuals. Within an organization, you have a natural motivation to complete the goal. A boss and colleagues will typically push each other to accomplish the goal. Failing that, there is the carrot-and-stick approach, where if you don't complete your goal, you could be fired, and if you do achieve it, there will be a bonus and perhaps a promotion.

When you set a SMART goal for yourself, you lose that accountability and motivation. You are on your own, and a SMART goal will do nothing for you when things get hard. Because there is no one in authority pushing you, it's too easy to give up, which is why, for example, having a personal trainer or an exercise partner is a much easier way to keep you going on a fitness program.

Setting goals is important for another reason: goals pull you out of your comfort zone. Getting stuck inside your comfort zone leads to stagnation and decline. While you may not want to change, the world around you is constantly changing, and it is on us to stay ahead, stay healthy, and adapt to the changing world.

As an aside, one of the most inspiring people I have ever spoken with was a 91-year-old gentleman in New York who asked me to help him set up his task manager. He was retired, and on the surface, my erroneous stereotypical ideas had me wondering why a 91-year-old wanted to learn how to use a task manager. We held the call on Zoom (he knew more about Zoom than I did!), and his enthusiasm for technology was awe-inspiring.

His life was full of activities and education. During our conversation, he told me he loved staying in touch with technology and learning new things because it kept him ahead of the changes going on in the world.

If SMART Goals Don't Work For An Individual, What *Does* Work?

If the part missing from SMART goals is the motivation part, this means you need to find your reason (why) you want to achieve a goal. That reason will motivate you and pull you through when things get hard. At the same time, you want to change old habits that no longer serve you and develop new habits that will move you forward without feeling like a drag.

One place you could start is with five simple questions. These questions came from Jim Rohn, a grandfather of the modern self-development world. These questions are designed to get you to think beyond the next few months or years. The questions are:

- What do I want to do?
- Who do I want to be?
- What do I want to see?
- What do I want to have?
- Where do I want to go?

These questions relate to your areas of focus in many ways. For example, what do you want to see? That would connect to your lifestyle and life experiences area, as would what you want to have and where you want to go.

Let's break these down.

What do I want to do?

This does not just relate to your career; it also relates to the things you want to do outside work. Go skydiving, drive a World Rally Championship car, learn to ride a horse, learn dry-stone walling, complete an Iron Man Triathlon, do amateur dramatics, write a book, or start a podcast. The list is endless.

Who do I want to be?

What kind of person would you like to be? Be careful here; it's easy to come up with standard adjectives to describe something. You want to be thinking in terms of who you really want to be. Being generous, kind, and loving is likely to be top of everyone's list. But what about hardworking, curious, organized, diligent, relaxed, minimalist, inspiring to others, charitable, strong leader, healthy, fit, and strong?

There are countless adjectives you could use to describe the kind of person you would like to be. To become that person, what are the traits you could adopt?

What do I want to see?

Similar to the question of where you would like to go, but more specifically, things you would like to see. Perhaps you would like to see the Northern Lights in Tromso, Norway, or Victoria Falls in Zimbabwe. The world is an astonishing place with so many incredible spots; let your imagination run wild.

What do I want to have?

This is the material question. Ignore the people who are anti-materialistic; setting a goal to buy an expensive watch or perhaps a boat can add a little spice to your life, and materialist things can be very motivating. It's true they rarely bring fulfilment, but as long as you are working on other areas in your life, then a few materialistic goals will not harm you in any way.

Where would you like to go?

Have you considered some unusual places you would like to visit? For instance, on my list are the locations where James Bond movies have been filmed, from Jamaica and Vietnam to Senna and Cortina in Italy. (Living in Korea, I have already visited the DMZ between North and South Korea). My wife would like to visit the villa used in the film Mama Mia, and my mother would love to visit Guadeloupe, where the BBC crime drama *Death in Paradise* is filmed.

If you struggle to come up with some ideas, there is a more powerful way to discover what you want, and that is to ask yourself who you envy.

Envy is a Really Good Motivator

Envy is where you see how someone else lives and want to have the same. *Jealousy*, on the other hand, is bad. Jealousy is where you believe it's unfair that someone else has something you do not have. Jealousy leads to bitterness and excuses. Envy gives you inspiration and motivates you to work hard and do things differently. It's the "if they can do it, so can I" mentality.

While initially, you may find that material things such as a house, a car or an expensive watch are motivating, in the long term they don't necessarily bring you happiness. After all, once you have that house or car or watch, what then? They don't change you by themselves, but the journey to acquiring them will change you.

> *"Become a millionaire not for the million dollars, but for what it will make of you to achieve it."* – Jim Rohn

What kind of person lives in your ideal home? What kind of person drives the car you want? These questions move you towards discovering the changes you will have to make in your life for you to achieve those things.

I envy Tony Robbins. He runs multiple companies, has helped and inspired millions of people worldwide, and lives an extraordinarily disciplined life. He's in a state of constant and never-ending improvement and has a loving and caring family.

This means all I need to do is look at Tony Robbins' life and analyze how he has built his life. How did he start? How did he create his programs? Collecting that knowledge will give me a blueprint I can use to build my own life and develop a set of goals.

I also envy people like Dwayne "The Rock" Johnson. Why? Because of his incredible self-discipline and energy. To maintain his physical health as he does, he exercises six to seven times a week and is meticulous about his diet.

In looking at people like Tony Robbins and Dwayne Johnson, I can learn what it takes to build a successful business, maintain my physical health and live with discipline. It's this knowledge that I can develop my own goals around. I discover the habits I need to adopt, the habits I need to change, and the strategies to build my own business that will help millions of people.

It is within these areas I can build my own goals – goals that will motivate and inspire me. On days when I am tired and "not in the mood" to write, I can remind myself that Tony Robbins would never let his mood stop him from helping people. If I don't feel like going to the gym, Dwayne Johnson reminds me that to be fit, strong and healthy, you never skip a gym session.

No matter what you want in life, someone somewhere is living that life. All you need to do is find them, digitally stalk them (the legal variety, not the illegal type), and learn what they have done to get there. That will give you a blueprint for what you need to change about how you live your life.

When I was a teenager, I admired Sebastian Coe, the then World record holder for the 800 and 1,500 meters. I read Athletics Weekly and Runners World religiously, looking to see how Sebastian Coe trained (there was no Google in those days) – how many times a week did he train on the track? When did he do his long runs? I built similar training programs into my training. As a result, I achieved a relatively high level of athletic success, representing my county at 1,500 meters in the English Schools Championships.

There's a wonderful story Sebastian Coe wrote in a Telegraph Newspaper article in 2009 about his Christmas Day training in 1979:

"It was a harsh winter (harsh enough to bring down a government), but I ran 12 miles on Christmas morning. It was a hard session, and I got home, showered, and felt pretty happy with what I had done.

"Later that afternoon, sitting back after Christmas lunch, I began to feel uneasy but was not quite sure why. Suddenly, it dawned on me. I thought: 'I bet [Steve] Ovett's out there doing his second training session of the day'. I put the kit back on, faced the snow and ice and did a second training session. I ran several miles, including some hill work.

"Not long ago, over supper in Melbourne, I told him the story. He laughed. 'Did you only go out twice that day?' he asked".

That's how powerful finding the people who inspire you and discovering their habits and practices can be.

Today, people like Rich Roll, Mel Robbins, Wim Hoff, Robin Sharma and David Goggins provide me with my blueprint. All highly disciplined people who want to help other people achieve their very best. It's their self-discipline and helping people to achieve their very best that inspires me. It motivates me every day, and I know I can do it. I can see a pathway: I know what to do because others have led the way. It's taught me what I must change about myself and what I must do each day.

Homework

So, who are the people *you* envy? The people doing what you want to do? Research how they did it. Read articles, watch interviews, and learn what they did to become the person they are today. While you are not trying to *be* them – you want to remain who you are – their mindset, habits, and routines will tell you what you need to do to become like them so you can achieve the things you want for yourself and others.

It's the blueprint you discover from researching these people that will give you the *what* and the *how* of your goals. It will also give you the behaviors you either need to change or adopt.

Create a note in your notes app and list out the qualities, habits and daily practices that got these people to where they are today.

As James Clear wrote in his book *Atomic Habits*:

> *"Once you have a handle on the type of person you want to be, you can begin taking small steps to reinforce your desired identity. I have a friend who lost over 100 pounds by asking herself, "What would a healthy person do?" All day long, she would use this question as a guide. Would a healthy person walk or take a cab? Would a healthy person order a burrito or a salad?"*

Building Discipline (And You're Going To Need It)

I've observed over the years that people who live a well-structured, disciplined life are often the happiest in society. There's something in the human condition that a sense of accomplishment and satisfaction leads to a state of happiness.

Many of those people practice meditation. If you have ever decided to take up meditation, you will likely have found sitting down to meditate difficult in the first week or two. You doubt yourself – "am I really meditating? – and when sitting quietly, ten minutes can feel like an hour. But if you stick with it for a week or longer, it gets easier. You begin to feel comfortable, and you start to feel the benefits. That consistency brings momentum, and before long you are looking forward to your meditation sessions.

That joy and accomplishment motivates you to continue, and again, you see the results, and, suddenly, you are in a cycle of success.

Now, let's flip that: you start your meditation program, but on the first day, you only manage two minutes before your phone beeped with an "urgent" notification. So you stop and give up. How do you feel at the end of the day?

You probably feel deflated, frustrated with yourself, and unhappy. Repeat that too many days, and you will search for excuses about how you can't do this and that you always fail at achieving your goals. In this state, how do you feel?

Jim Rohn and Tony Robbins regularly speak about which "pain" you choose for the day. "We can choose the pain of discipline or the pain of regret." Either way, you have to decide.

It's hard to wake up in the morning, and consistently stretch, meditate, or read a book. But equally, it can be hard to come home at the end of the day and know that you let yourself down, that you did not live up to the expectations you had of yourself.

However, there is something about the "pain of discipline," and that is the so-called "pain" is fleeting. Waking up to head out the door for a morning exercise session, the pain part is getting out of bed. But, once you get outside and begin, the pain disappears. You just get on and do it. Within a few minutes, that sense of achievement arrives, puts a smile on your face, and before you know it, you are enjoying yourself.

You get back home, jump in the shower, and a sense of pride in yourself takes over; you're smiling now, and that smile doesn't leave you all day. You did something hard for yourself.

It doesn't have to be about exercise, meditation, or reading. It could be doing your morning routine religiously every day. You may write a journal or spend a little time on yourself. Or it could be you no longer eat processed foods.

The pain of saying "no" to fast food or to your excuse for not meditating can leave you feeling a lot happier at the end of the day because you were being true to yourself and sticking to your values and principles.

And that is what it is all about – pursuing a disciplined life. Having a set of principles and values built into your life makes you feel accomplished at the end of each day.

Living a disciplined and structured life is not dull; that's something said by those who refuse even to try to live a structured life. A disciplined life is full of excitement because you are achieving things. You are learning what you are capable of doing, and you are moving forward toward building a life of passion, excitement, and inspiration, unlike an undisciplined life with the constant feeling of disappointment in letting ourselves down. And in trying to dull the pain of regret by indulging in escapist television shows or movies, looking at successful people, and finding excuses why you cannot be like them.

It will always come back to our choice each day: The choice between the two pains. I can promise you that if you choose the pain of discipline over the pain of regret, you will find you start to live a happier, more fulfilling life. And there is nothing more satisfying than reaching the end of the day knowing you did the hard things and won.

How Does This Work in the Time Sector System?

Once you have decided what needs to change to become the person you want to become, think about what you would need to do to make that happen. For instance, if you are inspired by those who wake up early and go to the gym or out for a run, you could open up your calendar and block an hour each morning for exercise.

Whatever you are trying to change, start slow. It's not about going out and exhausting yourself. It's about establishing the habit. You could spend the next six months going out for an early morning walk for thirty minutes. It's less about what you do; it's more about repeating the process day after day. That is how you develop habits. That is how you change behaviors. You could begin with five minutes of writing in a journal, or five minutes doing some morning stretches. There's no rush here. You are building a life, not a short-term fix.

Initially, there will likely be some trial and error; we rarely get things right the first time. You may find you need to play around with your wake-up times and how long you spend doing the activity you want to add. That's not failure, that's learning.

What about other goals you may want to accomplish? Perhaps you'd like to read more every day. Once again, this is less about how much you read; it's about developing the habit of reading. It's claimed Warren Buffett reads four to six hours a day, but does he do it every day? I'm sure there are days when he does not read that long. But it's clear from interviews with him he is a habitual reader. If your goal is to become a habitual reader (linked to your self-development area of focus), when will you read each day?

What about something a little more conceptual? Imagine you wish to become more disciplined. How could you create a goal around becoming more disciplined? Discipline is not tangible and can be difficult to measure. However, building discipline is similar to building muscle; the more you practice, the stronger it becomes. And as with building muscle, the way to do it is to start small.

Former US Special Forces Commander, Admiral William McRaven, said in his Texas University Commencement Address in 2014:

"If you make your bed every morning, you will have accomplished the first task of the day. It will give you a small sense of pride, and it will encourage you to do another task and another and another."

While this was about starting the day well, it can also be used to build your self-discipline. Making your bed in the morning may only be a two-minute task, but by being consistent with it and being deliberate in your actions, you are beginning the day by exercising your self-discipline.

Another way to develop self-discipline is to adopt Mel Robbins' Five-Second Rule: if you don't feel like doing something you know you should, count to five and then immediately do it. Mel mentions she learned this trick when she wanted to improve her discipline in getting out of bed in the morning without hitting the snooze button. Next time you are sitting on the sofa, and you have a sink full of dishes you know you should wash but just can't be bothered, stop, count to five, and immediately get off the sofa and head to the kitchen. It's so simple but works brilliantly.

To bring goals into your Time Sector System, what are the actionable steps you have identified? With meditation, your sessions go into your calendar – meditating is an appointment with yourself that usually involves being in a specific place. Reading can be added to your task manager as a recurring daily task until it becomes a habit. Once you have the habit, you can decide whether to keep it there or remove it.

What about longer-term goals? Career or financial goals? If you consider these, you will notice that to achieve them, there will be actions you need to take consistently. Saving a given amount of money is not achieved in one step; it's achieved by consistent action – such as sending an amount of money to a savings account each month. Similarly, becoming the CEO of a company is not achieved instantly; it can take years of training. You may decide you need to take an MBA course that will require consistent action from you to study. This study time can be put into your calendar.

So, sending money to your savings account each month would be a single task in your areas of focus folder (linked to your finance area): "Send $X.XX to savings account" and set to repeat on the same day each month. For your study time, you could set aside 8:00 pm to 10:00 pm each weekday evening for studying. This would be a block in your calendar called "study time." This will depend on how much time you are prepared to dedicate to studying.

Having goals is good because they give you a sense of purpose. To make a goal worthwhile, you must treat it as a catalyst for change. It's an engine burn to put you on the right course. Effective, motivating goals should be linked to at least one of your areas of focus, whether that is your health, your career or even a lifestyle change such as moving to a bigger home.

Your areas of focus, core work and goals are the foundations of your system. By giving yourself time to establish what these are and within your areas of focus what they mean to you, you are setting solid foundations for your system.

You would never build a home from the roof down; you build from the foundations up, and that is the same with building a sustainable productivity system. If you take the time to establish what your areas of focus, core work and goals are, you have the building blocks on which to create the life you want to live.

In the next section of the book, we will look at what tools can help you build your system, how to get the most out of them and how to implement the Time Sector System.

Homework

Go through your areas of focus again and ask yourself, on a scale of 1 to 10 how you are doing (with 1 being very bad and 10 being perfect). Take the three lowest scores and think what goals you could set for yourself to get these up to at least a 7.

Then, add the associated action steps either to your calendar or task manager and set them to recur as often as needed.

9

Using The Time Sectors

"You can't be thinking of everything you have to do at one time. You have to concentrate on just one thing at a time – one project, one job. You have to take it one task at a time. Do what you've set out to do. Keep your mind only on that one task. Why? If you don't, you won't accomplish anything." – Jim Rohn

In this chapter, we are going to look at how to use the time sectors in your task manager.

While your notes app will be where you work on your projects, your task manager is the place where everything starts. This is where you set the action of the work you need to do. Your notes app will carry the details, and your calendar will tell you if you have time to do it.

If you haven't already set up the Time Sector folders in your task manager, now is a good time to set them up.

When setting these up, the best place to begin is with your recurring tasks, and of these, the easiest one is *routines*. Routines are the things we need to do to maintain our life where it is. It's paying bills, taking the rubbish out, washing the car, cleaning your home and other recurring chores that just need to be done on a specific day. It would not be a catastrophe if you didn't clean your home on the day that task turns up, and that is the nature of what a routine task is: it would be nice to complete the task on the assigned day, but it wouldn't be a problem if you skipped it. In essence, this folder is to remind you these little "life" tasks need to be done.

While you can add a complete list of everything, I find dividing this folder into three areas helps keep things clean and tight and also makes reviewing this list from time to time easier.

Create three sections or sub-folders for daily, weekly, and monthly recurring routines. If you have annual routines, things like renewing your car or home insurance or making an appointment for your six-monthly dental check-up, you can put these in your monthly routines list.

How to Write Your Tasks

Before you do that, think about how you will write your tasks. Writing something like "garbage" or "Mortgage" may make sense to you right now, but next month on your daily list, this may not seem so clear. Always write your tasks with an action verb, something like *write, take, call, pay, send, review*, etc. So, for your mortgage payment, you would write "pay the mortgage," and for your garbage, you would write "take the garbage out."

Tasks without an action verb tend to be ignored or rescheduled. There's something about action verbs that gives a task power. This also helps when your energy levels are low or you are not in the mood to do the task.

"Put lawn mower away" is a better-written task than "lawn mower," or "clean up living room" is better than "living room" or "do the cleaning."

The problem with a task like "do cleaning" is it is not specific enough and makes the task appear bigger than it likely is. Be specific about what needs to be cleaned. When you see a task like "clean kitchen," you are much more likely to know exactly what needs to be done, and you will be more motivated to do it.

Think About and Decide on Tasks (Covert Procrastination Warning!)

There are many reasons why you may want to reschedule a task; it could be you ran out of time, or an emergency took over your day – all valid reasons. However, there is another reason why, and it's one I've found to be the most common.

Writing a task such as "Mum's birthday" or "Upload file" may make sense when you write the task. Give it two or three days, and when you see the task, you will hesitate. You need to remind yourself what it means. Leave it for longer than a week, and a task like this will make little or no sense. You won't remember what your intentions were when you wrote the task.

This is why when writing a task, you write for your "dumb" self while being your "intelligent" self. This means you make it very clear what you mean and precisely what the action is when you write the task.

However, you will likely put a type of task into your task manager that isn't a task. These tasks begin with words such as "think about" or "decide."

A "think about" task is not a task. Well, it's not a clearly defined actionable task with an ending. You could spend the next ten years thinking about something and doing nothing about it. A task like this will be one of the first things you kick down the road.

Similarly, a task that begins "decide" will deceive you. How much time does it take to make a decision? The answer? No time. You could make a decision instantly if you chose to do so. When you put a task like this in your task manager, it's a procrastination task. There's a reason why you have not decided on this, and *that* is what the real task is. You may need more information or need to discuss the options with a partner or colleague. Either way that is the real task.

Let's go back to the "think about" task. Where do you do your best thinking? It won't be sitting at your desk staring at a computer screen. You may think better when moving. It could be when you are out walking or driving. That's where you are likely to do your best thinking. For me, it's when I'm walking my dog, Louis.

A thinking task means you need more information. A real task here would be "read article about subject" or "ask Beverly how best to do this." That's actionable. "Think about" tasks are deceptive because there's no real action involved, and there's no definitive ending. You could "think" about this for eternity. Why are you "thinking about" it in the first place? The answer to that question will give you the real task.

Your tasks in your task manager should be clearly actionable so you don't waste time thinking about what you mean or what needs to be done. When writing the task, if you do the initial hard work and make sure it is clear and actionable, you will be less likely to reschedule it and, more importantly, procrastinate less. Rather than looking at a task and going "I don't know what to do," you'll decide whether to do the task based on your available time.

Sometimes, the difficulties you face with your task manager can be resolved with minor tweaks. It's unlikely you need any major restructuring; simply look at how you write your tasks. When you look at a task, do you instantly know what needs to be done? If the answer is *yes*, you've got it. If not, then consider rewriting the task so it is clear.

Now, when do these routine tasks need to be done? Imagine your rubbish is collected every Tuesday and Friday morning. So, you would need a recurring routine task that repeats every Monday and Thursday. That way, you would be alerted to take your rubbish out on those days.

Where you put a task like this is up to you. For me, if a task needs to be done twice a week, I will put it in my weekly section. If it needs to be done five or more times a week, then it would go into my daily section.

For instance, I have a routine task to review sales each day. That's done every day, so the task "Review today's sales" is in my daily routines section.

I also ensure my credit card is paid each month, and I have a recurring monthly task for paying my credit card. So, on the 16th, a task comes up that says: pay my credit card tomorrow.

In the first few weeks, you will likely find you will be adding quite a few routine tasks. That's perfectly normal. We are often not aware of the things we need to do as routines. For instance, I have a weekly routine task for my car maintenance. This normally involves nothing more complicated than checking the windscreen washer fluid levels and topping them up. It can be very annoying if you are caught out driving on an expressway many miles away from home, and the road is slightly wet with a lot of dirty spray being thrown up by the big trucks, and you hear the sound of your screen washer motor, but nothing coming out. You will thank yourself for a task like this.

Other routines may not be so obvious at first. So, be aware of what you are routinely doing, and if you feel you need a reminder, add it to your routines folder.

Look For Natural Triggers First

Avoid filling your task manager and calendar with tasks and events that do not need to be there. If you do something every day or week, or month without the need for a reminder, don't feel obligated to get it into your system. Personally, I don't need to remind myself to put my garbage bins out each week. There's a natural trigger. All my neighbors put theirs out. When I see their bins are out, I remember to take mine out.

Natural triggers are things in your environment that alert you that something needs doing. Putting fuel in your car, for instance, has a natural trigger; the fuel warning light will come on a few miles before you run out of fuel. Seeing a full laundry basket or an untidy living room may also act as a natural trigger for you to do some laundry or clean the living room.

There are also things you've been doing for years and would feel uncomfortable if you did not do them. Brushing your teeth in the morning and evening is one example. These types of tasks should not need to be on a task list. We brush our teeth naturally. We don't need reminding to do this. Likewise, make breakfast; if this is something you do every day, then you will be reminded to do it when you feel hungry.

Use natural triggers to your advantage. The less you have in your task manager, the better. Most people stop using task managers not because they don't work but because they are not curated and managed. The less in there, the less likely it will become overwhelming.

Recurring Areas Of Focus

This is the most important area of your task manager. This is where tasks that are meaningful and important to you and move your goals forward should go. These are very different from routine tasks because these tasks are critical. At a basic level, they ensure you regularly contact the people you care about, remind you to do your exercise, take your kids to the park, send money to your savings account, and remain focused on your long-term plans.

You can also put your core work tasks in your recurring areas of focus. This may seem counterintuitive, but when you are doing your work, it can be easy to lose track of the work you are paid to do. If you are in sales, and you are given a target to make contact with ten prospects each day, this is where you would put that task, "Contact ten prospects." If you are a writer, you may have a task that says, "Write 1,500 words" or "Write the first draft of blog post."

Imagine a person responsible for marketing in a small company. Their role is to create new content to post on social media each week. Their core work might look something like this:

- Monday - write the first draft of this week's blog post.

- Tuesday - write this week's newsletter and edit blog post.

- Wednesday - prepare five images for Instagram, post this week's blog post and edit the newsletter.

- Thursday – Send out this week's newsletter.

- Friday – Schedule next week's Instagram posts.

All these tasks would come up in their recurring areas of focus on the appropriate day. These are prioritized tasks. They are part of their core work and MUST be done each week. If they did not prioritize these tasks, their core work would not get done.

You may have noticed there are specific days to do the core work tasks; this helps to create a process. Having a process creates an automated workflow. When you begin your week, most of the time will be spent creating content (core work task). Doing things this way avoids having to think too much about how you will be spending your days, and it guarantees your core work gets done each week.

To make this more concrete you could use your calendar to block time for these activities. For example, on Monday and Tuesday, I have two hours in the morning blocked out for core work activities.. The only thing you need to know is between 9:30 am and 11:30 am on Monday you will be doing important work.

For longer-term plans and goals, you will find on a day-to-day basis, there is little you need to do. You will find for a financial goal, you may have a task that reminds you to send money to your savings account or arrange a quarterly call with your financial advisor. These tasks don't come up weekly, but it's still a good idea to have them in your recurring areas of focus to ensure you are moving these goals and areas forward.

When you read the chapter on Areas of Focus, if you did the exercise, you would have a clarifying statement for each of the eight areas. You will also have a list of steps you can take to ensure you are maintaining these important areas. Go through those steps and pull out any you need to do on a regular basis. For instance, if in your career and business area of focus, your clarifying statement outlines your career goal and the associated tasks include "set up a quarterly meeting with HR to discuss progress," this can be transferred to your recurring areas of focus.

You identified these tasks as being important to you. Therefore, they need to be recurring , so you are either moving things forward or you are maintaining them.

Many of your project tasks will be going into the time sectors, but there are some project tasks that may qualify for entry into your recurring areas of focus. These are the longer-term projects you are working on. If you have an important work project involving changing the payroll system for your global company that has been designated as a two-year project, there are likely to be a number of tasks that need to be done on a frequent basis. If you are in charge of this project, you may need to report progress to your boss on a consistent basis and arrange update meetings with your team. These recurring tasks can be placed inside your recurring areas of focus. The project is long-term and important, and these tasks are recurring tasks.

One-off tasks would not go in here. They would be placed inside one of the time sector folders. Your projects are being managed inside your notes app. However, to ensure your projects are moving forward, you can create tasks such as "work on Payroll project" in your recurring areas of focus. These bigger projects are, after all, projects you are focusing on, but often, they are slow-moving projects, so these recurring tasks serve as a way to make sure you are moving them forward appropriately each week and month. Once the project is complete, you can remove the task from your Recurring Areas of Focus.

Your Time Sector Folders

These will be self-explanatory. Any task you need to do this week will be placed inside your This Week folder. If the task does not need to be done this week, then the question to ask is: when does this task need to be done? If not this week, when? If you know a task needs to be done next week or sometime this month, you can put the task in the appropriate folder.

If you are working on a project and you realize a task needs doing but are not sure when you need to or even if you need to do it, then leave it in the project note. You have it; it's there, and you can highlight the task and add a note informing you to make a decision about it when the time comes. The tasks you have in your task manager are the tasks you know need doing, and you know roughly when they need doing. If the task is not in your This Week folder, then you can review it either each week or each month as required. The task is there, waiting for you to make a decision. If it's not going to be done this week, you don't need to worry about it.

Random Tasks

You are going to get some tasks that are not related to any projects or goals but just need doing. It could be you have been invited to give a brief talk at your next team meeting. You need to prepare a slide deck and an explanation about what you are working on. In this case, you add the task "prepare for team meeting talk" to your inbox, and later, when you process your inbox, you decide when you will have time to do that task.

Imagine in this scenario that you know you do not have time this week, so you push it off into the Next Week folder. Okay, you can now forget about that task. It's in your system, and you will see it when you do your weekly planning session, and you can decide then when you will do it.

Now, let's imagine you are informed on Friday that the team meeting you are to speak at is postponed until the 15th of next month. You can either move the task telling you to prepare for the meeting when you are informed or leave it until you do your next planning session.

When you do the weekly planning session, you will review your Next Week folder, and you can then decide when you will do the task. If it no longer needs doing next week, you can move it to your Next Month folder. You will review that folder in more detail at the end of the month.

You are also going to get a lot of tasks that need doing now or in the next few days; when processing your inbox, you can add these to the days you feel you have the time to do them. If they absolutely need to be done in the next twenty-four hours, but you currently don't have the time or space, you can decide what can be rescheduled so you have the time and space to complete them. You don't want to be locking everything in when you do the weekly plan; there will always be a need for flexibility, hence the reason why by doing a short daily planning session, you can assess what needs to be changed.

Long-Term and On Hold

This folder is for those tasks that you feel need to be done at some time, but either you are not sure when or, if you do know, they do not need to be done in the next three months or so. This is a holding pen for tasks you are not sure about yet or are on hold until sometime in the future.

This folder does not need to be reviewed often. I advise reviewing it every two to three months. You'll likely find that you delete more from this folder than move anything forward. Something that seems like a good idea today becomes a preposterous idea in two months' time.

The whole point of the Time Sector System is to remove from view anything you do not need to do this week. Most people's problems with time management and productivity in general are related to feeling overwhelmed. There's too much stuff to be done and too little time in which to do it. What we are doing with the Time Sector System is creating a process that manages the work you are doing on a day-to-day, week-to-week basis so you are focused on what is important this week and not having to worry about anything that may or may not come up next week.

Work is moving too fast for many of your tasks to still be relevant in two or three weeks' time. Some of those tasks will change, others will no longer need to be done, and some you will look at next week and wonder why you ever thought they were tasks in the first place.

When we are so caught up in our day-to-day tasks, we easily lose track of what is really important to us – our long-term goals and areas of focus. With the Time Sector System, these are the central part of your whole system. If your system were a solar system, your long-term goals and life purpose would be the sun – everything revolves around them. Your areas of focus would be your moon; they come around when they need to come around and help to keep you in stasis. And your projects would be those comets and asteroids that fly past at regular intervals that just need dealing with when they come around.

When you implement the Time Sector System, one of the advantages you will soon find is the speed at which you can get things processed into your system. Traditional time management and productivity systems typically require a lot of processing and organizing just to keep them operational. That may have been fine in the past; we had a little more time to do that. But these days, things are happening far too fast for us to spend a lot of time processing inboxes and organizing our tasks.

The Time Sector System only requires you to make a simple decision – when are you going to do this task? Now, there are likely to be a number of factors determining that, such as the deadline, who's asking you to do the task and how much time you have available this week. But these decisions are much easier to make than trying to decide whether a task is a single action related to a project or whether there are multiple steps involved, thus making it another project to manage.

The only things that matter today are the tasks you've decided need to be done today. That's where your focus should be.

It is going to take a few weeks for you to get used to this more minimalist approach to time management if you are coming to this from an older time management system. You may feel a little disoriented at first managing projects from your notes app but stick with it. As time goes by, you will find you become faster and more in tune with what you can realistically complete each week. You will also find you become more focused on what you are doing, because when you are working on a project, you won't be distracted by all the other little tasks for your other projects.

Processes vs. Projects

So far in this book, I've used the generic word "project" for groups of tasks that have a common outcome. It's a traditional way to view much of the work you do. However, is this the *best* way to view your work?

A few years ago, I discovered if I treated everything that involved two or more steps as a project (the traditional way of viewing groups of tasks), it changed how I felt about the work. It felt there was a need to plan things, create a list of tasks and choose a start date. All these steps are rendered obsolete when you have a *process*.

With processes, you only need to know when you will start the work. Because you have a process, you already know what needs to be done and can do it without excessive planning and preparation.

I would define a project as something one-off that requires multiple steps. A process, on the other hand, is something that you frequently do that requires multiple steps.

When Aston Martin, the car manufacturer, decided to build a high-performance SUV, it was a big departure from the usual cars they built. Aston Martin was famous for making sports cars and grand tourers. Their iconic DB5 – often called the James Bond car as it has been featured in many of the James Bond movies – could never be described as anything like an SUV!

With the decision to make an SUV, Aston Martin's management determined they would need to build a new factory. That became a project. The last time Aston Martin built a factory was many decades ago. There was no process for building factories.

Once the new factory was built, they set about developing the process for building the cars. Building a car is not a project; it's a process. If each new car were treated as a project, it would take too long to build, there would be too many decisions to be made, and it would be incredibly inefficient.

Within each new car build, there will be varying levels of extras to be added as well as color schemes, yet Aston Martin still follows a process. It's effective and efficient, and a problem can be quickly isolated and fixed if anything goes wrong.

If you were watching TV In the UK and Ireland, on January 1st you would notice something. The TV ads are no longer stores advertising their Christmas sales, instead they are all about holidays to places like Majorca, Ibiza, Greece, or Croatia. If you've ever been in the UK or Ireland on 1st January, you'd realize this was a smart move by the holiday companies. The weather outside is horrendous. Dark, cold, gloomy, and wet.

The number one reason for these ads in early January is because many families begin planning their summer holidays at the start of the year. There are discussions about where to go, what type of hotel to stay at, and for how long. Once a decision is made, someone will need to book the holiday.

Given that this is repeated every year, a process is being followed. An ad on TV triggers the discussion, a short list is agreed upon. A further discussion is then arranged to narrow down the shortlist to one destination. A search is done online one evening and a decision is made.

Then there is the discussion about who will book the holiday.

It's all a process. The same set of tasks are being followed every year and it's all triggered by the TV ads switching people's attention away from winter sales to the summer holidays.

No one is planning out in great detail the exact steps that need to be followed. It's not a project. It repeated at the same time each year therefore it is a process.

Building processes is not about having a single process. It's about creating multiple processes for the work you regularly do. That may sound very complex or difficult, but if you stop and think about it, you are already using processes for almost everything you do. Have you noticed when you wash your dishes after breakfast or dinner, you wash things in the same way? You don't stand there and have a meeting to decide what to wash first. It's likely the same when you prepare to go to bed. you brush your teeth and turn off all the lights before bed. It's the same process each day.

The great thing about processes is they become automatic. You don't think about each step involved in brushing your teeth or washing your dishes. You just do it.

(If you are lucky enough to have a dishwasher, notice how you place things in there. I bet you put things in the same order each time.)

The same applies to your work processes. You don't need to think about what to do; you follow the process.

Now, processes do not work for everything. A process is used for anything you may repeat frequently. It's unlikely you will redecorate your bedroom often. Doing a job like that will be a project. But what would it be if you were a painter and decorator? In that case, you would have a process for decorating different types of rooms. You will follow the same process when you begin painting a new room. Clear the furniture or cover it with dust sheets, wipe down the walls and set up your ladders, paint, and brushes. (That's a guess. I'm not a painter or decorator).

Ross Brawn, the former Ferrari Formula 1 technical director, developed a process for preparing the following year's car.

The FIA, Formula 1's governing body, would issue the technical directives for the following year at the end of March. Once he received them, he would use April to review the new rules and regulations. Then, there would be a week-long technical team meeting that began on the first Monday of May each year, where they would discuss the new regulations and allocate team members to start building the new car. By the beginning of the following week, they had started the new car build.

Each different department had a process for making whatever they were responsible for, be that the chassis, engine, or aerodynamics. Nothing was considered a project. It was a process that was followed each year.

Now, in Formula 1, the team's objective is very clear: to build a car that wins. No team goes into building a new car with the thought of coming second or third. They build to *win*. Motivating team members isn't particularly difficult.

Every Monday, there was a team meeting to discuss progress and to see where Ross Brawn, as the leader, could help to move things forward. But ultimately, everything was a process.

This quote from the book *Total Competition: Lessons in Strategy from Formula One*, by Ross Brawn and Adam Parr nails it for me:

> "Develop and apply a set of rhythms and routines. Having established an integrated team and structure, Ross instituted rhythms and routines that ensured the completeness of the process of designing, manufacturing, and racing cars. These routines constantly reinforced alignment around a shared vision."

That shared vision was to have a championship-winning car and driver.

The great thing about building processes is once you have established them, you can isolate areas where things are not working as well as you would like instead of having to rewrite a whole project.

For example, I developed my email management system through several refinements over several years. As the volume of emails increased, I found it increasingly difficult to stay on top. My old system, or process, for managing it no longer worked. I needed to look at the process and see how to improve it.

Collecting email was not a problem. That was a part I had no control over, but I did realize that part of the problem with volume was I was too ready to give out my email address to anyone who asked for it. I soon realized that my email address was ending up in databases, which was part of the problem.

So, I created a new email address for all non-important occasions when I needed an email address and kept that as webmail only.

Then, I looked at how I was processing mail, which led to my Inbox Zero 2.0 system. It was a refined version of Merlin Mann's original Inbox Zero methodology. It works effortlessly now and has never let me down since I modified the process around ten years ago. Shortly I will give you that process when we come to managing email and other communications.

A good friend of mine is a copywriter in Korea. She's a brilliant copywriter, and each new job that comes her way follows the same process. She takes notes in Apple Notes when she meets the client for the first time. She finds out what they want, the tone of the words and anything else relevant.

Then, it gets added to her list of work as a task in Apple's Reminders. The task is simple: "Work on new client's job." And she works through her jobs in chronological order.

Working on the task means she opens Apple's Text Edit (a simple text editor built into Apple's computers) and does all her work there until she sends the first draft to the client.

Her whole process works. She's consistent and on time, making her life so easy. Her calendar is blocked out for focused work and client meetings, and she's strict about what goes on it. It's all a process. Never a project.

You see, the problem with projects is we waste so much time planning, organizing, and thinking about what we need to do. We feel obligated to write out what we think needs to happen, much of which does not need to be done anyway, and we then procrastinate about where and when to start.

With processes, you already know *where* to start, so you only need to decide *when* to start. There's no procrastinating because you already know the first step.

You also have a better idea of how long something will take. Processes are naturally broken down into different components, and the more you run that process, the more you learn how long something will take.

The best way to build processes is to track how you do different parts of your work. Where are the natural breaks? There will be a number of different parts: Decide on the topic, write the first draft, edit the first draft, select image, post. Five steps. If you repeat those steps week after week, it won't be long before you learn how long each part takes.

Keep things as simple as possible and look for the natural components. Then, build processes from there.

When you start looking for processes, you will realize turning everything into a project slows you down and is one of the most inefficient ways to get work done. Processes are efficient and only require a trigger to get started. With projects, you don't have a trigger, which leads to meetings and discussions on how to get things started.

With processes, you know the steps before you begin and can anticipate the time it will take to complete them; that gives you the proper foundation to complete your work on time every time.

Once you have established a process for doing your work, a great question to ask yourself is: *where can I improve this process?*

Japanese manufacturing companies are obsessed with finding what they call "the friction points" in a process. These are the parts of a process that slow things down or create issues. They are consistently looking for better and more effective ways to improve the manufacturing process. This is something you too can adopt.

The way to start this is to look at what you do and find the parts of your work you struggle with. Why do you struggle? Does it always take longer than you anticipate? It could be you are heavily reliant on other people, which means the outcome is delayed. What can you do to eliminate those delays?

One of the best things about looking for friction points in this way is that it makes even the most mundane parts of your work more interesting. The results often mean you turn something you once disliked doing into something you no longer dislike.

My client, the VP of his company's factory, identifies his core work as employee safety, factory productivity, and costs. This client has turned monitoring these areas into a process he completes daily at work. He begins by reviewing the accident reports and then checks the previous day's output and expenditures. Doing this daily takes him no more than twenty minutes because he knows where to get the information. From the information he gets from this process, he can determine his priorities for the day.

Fortunately, accidents involving his team are very rare. Still, if he notices a reduction in output, he knows to speak with the people responsible to see what went wrong and he can then, if necessary, develop a solution. Similarly, if costs have gone up, he can investigate and make decisions that will ultimately bring those costs down.

The advantage of using processes is that each time you run a process, you can see where things work and where they don't. You can also find parts you can eliminate.

Most people I speak with cite communications as the biggest drag on their productivity. Email and messages are persistent and part of our work that demands a process. How do you manage your communications? Do you allow notifications to interrupt you every time a new one comes in, or have you developed a better way? Allowing messages and emails to interrupt your work is a symptom of FOMO (Fear of missing out) and causes tremendous pain and stress on other parts of your work.

You could, for example, use the InBoxZero 2.0 methodology to deal with emails and set some rules of engagement with messages. Rules of engagement are a fantastic way to develop a process for managing Slack and Teams messages. For instance, you could make it a rule to never look at your phone while with a customer or while driving (and when visiting the bathroom – no, seriously, you can do this!). Then, once you have finished your meeting or arrived at your destination, you can give yourself five minutes to deal with any messages.

Don't accept the status quo of "my boss expects me to respond immediately." If you have a boss like that, it's time to talk with your boss. This is a sign of poor management, and poor managers never last long. However, you can explain your process to your boss, and as long as the reason you do not respond immediately is genuine, any decent boss would agree to your rules of engagement.

What could you do better if you took a few minutes to look at your process? If you want more time for other things and to improve your work, perhaps this question is worth asking.

Give Your Processes Time To Work

How long did it take you to learn to walk unaided when you were a child? How long did you have training wheels on your bike before you could ride a two-wheeled bike without falling off?

Most toddlers learn to walk by crawling first, then pulling themselves up on a chair, only to take a step and fall over. We have to repeat that process over and over again until one day, as if by magic, we can walk from one chair to the next without falling over.

The one thing you did not do was give up because you fell over. You picked yourself up and tried again. It's a tried and tested formula. Why don't we do that by building a productivity system?

There are several reasons why we feel our first attempt failed, so we have to find another solution. One of those will be seeing other people effortlessly get through their work each day without any issues.

Then there's the pernicious FOMO (Fear of Missing Out) we experience when our favorite YouTubers rave about another new notes app or task manager. Any one of these would make us feel uncomfortable and question our system.

Interestingly, if you watch carpenters or saddlers doing their work, the tools they use every day are old – very old. I've seen hundred-year-old scissors and fifty-year-old hammers and chisels being used by some of the most skilled people I've ever observed.

For your time management and productivity system to work effectively, give it time to mature. The steps you take to engage with your work each day should be part of a process you follow *every* day. When you repeat your process every day, you learn to use it effectively.

When I read David Allen's *Getting Things Done* for the first time, I realized that a weekly review was a massive part of becoming better at managing my work and time. That first weekly review I did took three hours! I followed the book's recommended checklist and meticulously went through every inbox, project, and note I had collected. I consciously had to think about each step. When I had finished, I was exhausted.

Yet, today, fourteen years later, my weekly review takes no more than forty minutes. I've repeated the process every week for fourteen years, with few exceptions, and I know exactly where to look; I can review projects without consciously thinking about the review process. It's automatic.

But it wasn't always automatic. Those first few reviews took hours. I was new to it; it was unfamiliar, and I had to think about each step.

The best productivity systems disappear into the background. From the moment you decide to do something, you put it into your inbox. From there, you process that task into your task manager, and the task appears on the day you plan to do it. Any additional steps only add complication and will ultimately slow you down.

There is a saying in the US and UK special forces, "slow is smooth, smooth is fast." This refers to practicing a process repeatedly until it becomes automatic and smooth. You will inevitably screw up, make mistakes, and drop the ball to get to the smooth stage. It's a repeated practice that will make you so smooth you become effortlessly fast at doing it.

You can read books and blogs and watch YouTube videos on productivity systems all day. At some point, though, you need to create your own system and make it work. All systems work, but each system needs work. So you have to make it work. A tremendous amount of energy and effort is required to build the necessary muscle memory and repetition for your system to work, but it's worth it. When doing your work becomes automatic, you can focus on being creative and doing the work itself rather than having to think about how to organize your work.

I recently watched an upholsterer sewing a cover onto a classic Egg Chair. The upholsterer explained what she was doing, and when she came to the final sewing, she said this was one of the most therapeutic parts of reupholstering. I watched in awe and imagined myself trying to do that sewing. It would be anything but therapeutic. But then, I don't have over twenty years of experience sewing every day. Slow is smooth, smooth is fast!

"Repetition is the mother of mastery," so give your new productivity system time to work. Repeat the process daily and make minor adjustments, but don't give up because it's hard work. It will be hard work, at first – you're changing habits and routines – but it will be worth it. Enjoy the journey because you'll become the standard-bearer for others to follow when it finally clicks.

Checklists

Once you have established processes for doing your work, you can create a checklist for each one. These checklists can then be saved in your resources section in your notes to be available whenever needed.

Checklists are the secret sauce to becoming more productive because they take the decision-making out of what to do next. No pilot would ever take off without going through the pre-flight and pre-takeoff checklists. Similarly, no surgeon would perform surgery without a checklist.

A few years ago, I went into a hospital for a hernia operation. Hernia operations are minor surgical procedures, yet I was being run through a checklist from the moment I entered the hospital. I had my blood taken for analysis, I was allocated a bed, the intravenous drip was attached, and that was the day before the surgery.

That night, a doctor came around and explained the procedure and potential dangers of the operation. I then signed the consent forms and tried to get to sleep.

My surgery was scheduled for 9:30 am, and at 8:00 am, a nurse took my blood pressure, checked the IV line, and began the first set of questions. My name, why I was in the hospital, and which side the hernia was on.

An orderly came to take me to the operating room around 9:15 am, and again, I was taken through a series of questions. Entering the surgical suite more questions, and finally, once I was on the operating table, I was taken through the questions, a nurse explained what would happen, and I fell asleep.

Talking with my surgeon after the operation, he explained why I was asked the same questions at each point. It was all part of the surgical checklist they followed with every patient. It reduced mistakes and ensured that everyone on the surgical team knew precisely what was happening and where they were on the checklist.

You Don't Have To Do Everything Today

One of the best things about using a to-do list is that it removes all the little things swirling around in your head that are preventing you from developing creative solutions to the many issues you face.

You spend all day burning mental energy worrying about everything you think you have to do, instead of having the mental space to come up with solutions. Getting all those things out and into an external place generates that space.

The flip side of that, though, is that once you do have everything swirling around in your mind out and into a list, your natural reaction is likely to feel you must get all those tasks done ASAP.

That is simply not true. Many of the items on your list can wait. If you want to become better at managing your time and be a lot less anxious and stressed, you need to break down that list to spread out the tasks you feel compelled to do.

Let's start with this premise: you cannot do everything in one day. So, the natural question is, what *can* you do in one day? This answer should be realistic and leave you feeling challenged but not exhausted. It's not about what you would *like* to do; it's about what you *can* do each day.

To get to this stage, know your essentials. For instance, if you were in sales, how many customers would you have to be in contact with each day at a very minimum? Likewise, if you are a teacher, how many classes do you have to teach and prepare for, as a minimum, each day?

In your personal life: what are the daily essentials for your relationships, hobbies (remember those?), and personal development?

Once you know what these are, you will know what time you have left for everything else. If you find you don't have any time left in the day after you have completed these, you should go back and get very strict about what you call "essential."

If you were a training manager in a large company, your "essentials" could be:

- Review workbook for the upcoming health and safety seminar (2 hours).

- Prepare joining instructions for participants (1 hour).

- Respond to my communications (1 hour).

- Take my dog out for a walk (90 mins).

- Write remaining employee evaluations (90 mins).

In total, your essentials would take 7 hours.

If you take out the one personal essential today, that leaves you with 5 ½ hours of focused work for today. That's certainly doable. Taking your dog out for a walk would be a nice break in the day.

If you build your daily to-do list around your essentials and ensure that they get done, you will feel far more fulfilled at the end of the day.

There will always be other things you would like to do in a day, but if you postpone those until another day, that would be fine. You start the day knowing that as long as you get those five things done, you will be on top of your work, get done your high-value tasks, and rest at the end of the day feeling satisfied and relaxed.

Once you know what your essentials are, you have built the foundations of a productive day. If you continue to randomly add tasks to your task manager in the false belief that everything on there is important, you will not only fail; you will fail AND be stressed out and overwhelmed!

Trying to do everything in one day (or week or month) is impossible. You could continue to fight it, but you will lose, and it will be a defeat that comes with a terrible cost to your health and future success in both your professional and personal life. That cost is too high.

If you are serious about becoming better organized and more productive, begin with your essentials. Then, fine-tune these until they are the absolute essentials, and ensure you have time allocated for them. Once that's done, you will know how much time you have left for the nonessentials, and you can, if you wish, work on those.

The great thing about knowing what your essentials are each day is that you still have time to deal with the unexpected -- those urgent demands from your boss or handling a dissatisfied customer. There's always time for those if your focus is on the essentials and you have done what you can to eliminate the nonessentials. Your problems will begin when you start prioritizing the nonessentials. It's then that things will quickly spiral out of control, and no to-do list is going to help you then.

> "At some point, you will have to learn to let go. There is an endless list of obligations and expectations, desires, and ambitions, and worries and fears that will always be ready to insert themselves between you and the feeling of peace. If you never learn to let them go, there will never be enough."
> **– James Clear**

Homework

Take a piece of paper (or create a new note in your notes app) and think about what you would consider to be your essential work. Must of this will come from your core work. What you are looking for are the tasks you need to perform each day.

This will help you identify your essentials on a day to day basis.

10
Planning Your Day

"Highly focused people do not leave their options open. They select their priorities and are comfortable ignoring the rest. If you commit to nothing, you'll be distracted by everything." – James Clear

So now you have everything set up. Your goals, areas of focus and core work are all established, and you know what you need to perform each day. How do you make sure that what you are doing each day is the right thing? That comes from doing a daily planning session.

It's the daily (and weekly) planning sessions that will add automation to your day and give you time each day to ensure that the direction you are heading is the direction you want to go.

The daily planning session is a ten to fifteen-minute planning session you perform at the end of the day. If you have set up your goals, areas of focus and core work as recurring tasks where appropriate, you will not need to do much with these. They will be coming up as and when they need to come up. What you are going to be looking at are the additional tasks you have collected through the day and looking at tasks you have scheduled and making sure they are still relevant.

However, what planning the day really means is prioritizing your day. Often, you find what you have planned for tomorrow is going to be more than you will be able to accomplish. Don't worry – this is perfectly normal. This is why you do the daily planning. You look at the list of tasks you have for tomorrow, and based on what your calendar is telling you about how many meetings you have and what commitments are scheduled, you can decide what you can get done.

Too often, people beat themselves up because they did not clear their task list for the day. It's as if they feel like they failed. Yet did they fail? No, of course they didn't.

You are, hopefully, a functioning human being. That means you are flawed because you have emotions and hormones, and perhaps you did not get enough sleep last night or had a heavy lunch. The one thing you are not is a machine. And that is what makes you special.

Over seven days, you will have some good days where you get a lot done and remain focused. You are also going to have some average days ("Meh days"). Days where you feel you are going through the motions slowly, but you do get stuff done. And you will have some bad days when getting anything done is a struggle.

Unfortunately, you cannot plan when you will have a good, meh, or bad day. They are random. However, what you can do is be aware of how you feel on a given day. Do your best with your energy and focus; at the end of the day, accept it for what it is.

You can reschedule anything you did not get around to and move on when you do your end-of-day planning. You did not fail. You just needed to reschedule some of your tasks, and that's fine. Tomorrow is a new day; if you need to catch up on your sleep, you can go to bed a little earlier today.

Improving our time management and productivity will always be a work in progress. We constantly seek ways to improve our processes, refine our structures and build our discipline. That's the great thing about being human: we can continuously adjust, correct, and improve at any time.

So, it's okay if you don't complete all your tasks today. Accept it was a meh or bad day and move on. Reschedule and be confident that tomorrow with be better.

One area many people find difficult is prioritizing their work. Prioritization is a skill that, with practice, you can become very good at. Treating everything you collect as being important will not work – if everything is important, then nothing is. You will never be able to do everything you want to or feel you must do. You have to prioritize!

Your goals, areas of focus, and core work will give you the majority of your priority tasks. The problem a lot of people find is they begin to treat these as low-priority tasks and move the loudest tasks to the top of their priority list.

This is a mistake. In fact, it is one of the biggest mistakes people make when creating a time management system.

There will be occasions where something that may not normally be a priority becomes a priority. That's fine – it happens. A big project enters its final week, and all hands need to be available to get it completed. You find you have an unusual number of emails that need prompt replies. There could be an emergency in your family that requires you to drop everything and deal with the emergency. While these "emergencies" hopefully will be rare, they do come up. The system you are building now is flexible enough to manage these, hopefully, rare occurrences.

So, how do you prioritize *your* day?

The 2+8 Prioritization Method

I devised the *2+8 Prioritization Method* because of a problem I was experiencing daily, and it will be one I am sure you have also faced: starting the day with an overwhelming list of tasks and not knowing where to begin. Once you begin prioritizing what is important to you first, you can then address the loud, shouting tasks. These tasks still need doing, but what it means is your core work gets done first.

To help you stay focused on what is important, the 2+8 Prioritization Method is a simple method that selects two objective tasks that MUST be completed each day (your "must-dos") and eight other tasks you will do whatever you can to complete. Now, the eight "should-do" tasks are important, but if you do not have time to complete them, it would not be a crisis. All you would do is reschedule these for another day.

At the end of the day, when you do your planning session, you look at your tasks for tomorrow and decide which two tasks are not negotiable. They MUST be done whatever it takes. You flag these or highlight them in whatever way you can to make sure they are at the top of your list. You then select the eight other tasks you feel *should* be done. Again, you want some way to highlight these so you can see them clearly.

Depending on what task manager you are using, it is helpful to separate these from your other tasks. This list will be the main list you will work on for most of your day. You can do this through tags or flags. If your task manager does not have tags (labels) or flags, then you can create a folder and call it "Today's focus" and move your ten tasks into this folder.

Another way of doing this is to use a small notebook. As you begin your day, take two minutes to write down your two MUST DO tasks, and the eight other things you would like to get done that day. Keep this little notebook on your desk open at today's date. As you complete your tasks, cross them out.

The motivation you get seeing your daily list getting crossed out will aid your focus for the day and prevent you from being tempted by easier tasks that may be lurking in your digital task list.

This method does *not* mean you only work on ten tasks per day. You would not include your routines in here unless one of these had become a priority. For instance, on a weekend, you may decide that cleaning up your home is a priority, and you can add that to your 2+8. But in principle, the tasks you prioritize each day are those tasks that you have decided are important.

At the end of the day, before you close down your computer and stop work, look at your tasks for tomorrow and select your two objective (must-do) tasks. Then, select your eight should-do tasks.

Review your calendar for your events. It's surprising how many people are caught out by long-forgotten early morning meetings. Make sure you know where you need to be and when first thing in the morning. Then close down your computer. Your day is planned.

The benefits of doing this are huge. First, you reduce stress because you get whatever's on your mind off your mind. You know where you need to be tomorrow, and you know you have the time needed to get whatever work you want to do done.

Secondly, it instructs your subconscious mind to do its thing, and that is to prepare you for the work ahead. Your subconscious mind is incredibly powerful. It uses your learned knowledge and experiences to deliver solutions to difficult problems. The trouble with our subconscious mind is it can be slow. It needs time to do its work. Conversely, our conscious mind is incredibly fast. It evolved to anticipate danger and will trigger our fight-or-flight responses very quickly.

Our subconscious minds do not work in that way. Our subconscious mind is the slow, pondering mind, and yet if you give it enough time – a night's sleep, for example – you'll often find when you wake in the morning, any difficult problems you may have been searching solutions for are no longer difficult problems.

This is why your daily planning is best done the day before. It sets you up for the next day and it means you are not wasting valuable time trying to decide what to do when you are likely to be at your freshest and most focused.

Try this experiment this evening: take something you are struggling with – it could be a difficult problem you are trying to solve, or to come up with ways to kick-start a stalled project, and consciously ask yourself what you could do to solve this problem. Then sleep on it.

While it is not guaranteed, the chances are you will wake up in the morning with ideas on resolving whatever is bothering you. You may need to do this over a few evenings, but eventually, your slow, subconscious mind will deliver you some fantastic ideas. It's like your very own personal ChatGPT built into your brain. It takes all your stored knowledge and experiences and uses that to give you a set of results.

The strange thing is many people struggle to find these ten to fifteen minutes at the end of the day. This means they skip the daily planning and end up wasting valuable time at the start of the next day trying to figure out what to do.

Peter Drucker, the eminent economics and management professor, in his classic book *Management Challenges for The 21ˢᵗ Century*, described a knowledge worker as a person who needed to define their work. This is very different to an assembly line worker, who has a clearly defined set of tasks that are performed repeatedly throughout a shift. A knowledge worker needs to decide what to work on from a long list of ill-defined tasks and then get on and do that work. If you can make that decision before you end the previous day, you not only begin the day with a clear set of tasks, but you will also have engaged your subconscious mind in the process, making the tasks a lot easier to perform.

The Ivy Lee Method

Most desk diaries only have space for around six tasks at the bottom of each day's column. Ironically, six was the number Ivy Lee recommended when he devised the Ivy Lee method for Bethlehem Steel in 1918. That method worked then, and it still works today.

One of the founders of Bethlehem Steel, Charles M Schwab, commissioned Ivy Lee, a successful public relations entrepreneur to find a way to improve the productivity of his senior managers. Ivy Lee asked to speak with each manager, and he gave each of them the same piece of advice:

At the end of the day, write down, in order of priority, the six tasks you want to complete tomorrow. Leave that piece of paper on your desk so when you arrive back at work in the morning, the first thing you see are those six tasks. Then, you begin at the top and work your way down the list until you have all six crossed out.

Think about that for a moment. How confident would you be in being able to complete six tasks each day consistently?

Let's imagine for a moment you are a university professor. Today, you have two ninety-minute lectures to give beginning at 9:00 am. Your lectures will finish at 12:15 pm, and then you have to arrange some meetings with your Ph.D. students, mark some papers, spend a little time writing your own paper, respond to your email, prepare for your lectures tomorrow, and exercise. That's six tasks. Do you have time for anything else? If you work a typical eight or nine-hour day, three hours have already taken lecturing, which leaves you with five to six hours to do everything else.

Exercise can be done after you finish for the day, but marking papers, writing your own paper, and responding to emails are not five-minute tasks. If you try and cram anything else into your day, you've lost the day.

The difficulty with not planning the day before is that when you try to plan the day the next day, you will soon find you will be distracted. You'll probably check email and Slack messages and engage in gossip with your colleagues. When you start the day knowing exactly what it is you want to accomplish, you are going to be much more focused and a lot less likely to be distracted by other things.

You should make your daily planning session a non-negotiable part of your day. It's just ten to fifteen minutes. If your workday ends at 6 pm, then start closing down at 5:30 pm. This gives you enough time to make sure you have not missed any important messages, allows you time to clean up your work for the day, and then review tomorrow's appointments, review your task list, and do your 2+8 prioritization.

The 2+8 Prioritization Method is not just about your work. Imagine you are coming to the closing training sessions for a triathlon you have been preparing for all year. These final few training sessions are important. You can make your training sessions an objective task for the day – remember, objectives are your MUST-DO tasks for the day.

Another advantage you will have from doing your planning the day before is you will sleep a lot better. This planning calms your over-active conscious mind. It reassures it that you have everything under control and that there are no fires developing that will become a crisis to deal with tomorrow.

As you have set your Recurring Areas of Focus and Routines up as recurring tasks, these will be pulled into your daily list automatically. This means when you do your daily planning, many of your tasks will already be populating your list for tomorrow. You will also likely have a number of one-off tasks that you will have scheduled when you did your weekly planning session (see next chapter). This means all you are doing when you do a daily planning session is deciding which of your tasks for tomorrow are your MUST-DO or SHOULD-DO tasks.

How you decide these will come down to a number of factors: time sensitivity – when the task's deadline is, urgency, whether it is a goal task or an area of focus, or who's asking you to do the task.

You will find a lot of your daily planning will involve rescheduling tasks. That's normal, and you should not feel guilty about it. You are making a decision and being intentional (and realistic) about your time; that's far better than being unrealistic and just ignoring everything on your list when you realize you don't have enough time. That would make your whole system meaningless, you won't trust it, and you will be wasting your time. To give you a benchmark, I find on average, most people reschedule around 30-40% of their tasks each day. If you are in the same range, don't worry about it. You're not failing; you're being realistic.

Try to avoid overthinking things and allowing your daily planning to take too long. The goal is to get it done in ten minutes or less, and with practice, this will be perfectly achievable. If you are taking longer than twenty minutes, you are reviewing too much. With daily planning, you only need to decide what you will and will not do tomorrow. That's it!

Your daily planning session gives you time to focus on the important things and sets you up for a much more relaxing evening, knowing you have everything under control. It's about accepting what you did, looking at tomorrow, and deciding what needs to be done.

It's Not About Doing More

Have you ever asked yourself why you want to become more productive and better manage your time? If your reasons are about *doing more*, you may have grasped the wrong end of the stick.

The goal of improving your productivity and time management should always be to do *less*. This may, at first, sound strange; surely, being more productive means doing more in less time. In a corporate context, that may be true. However, in a personal context, it's about doing what you have to do in less time to have more choices about what you could do.

Becoming better organized is about giving yourself the space and time to decide what you want to do and what can be discarded.

This means that rather than doing more work, you search for better ways to do it, so it takes less effort and time. That could mean you look at your processes to see where you can fine-tune them. Or it could be you analyze where and why you procrastinate – a lack of sleep, poor diet choices or being a little too social with your colleagues, for instance.

It also means carefully curating your daily list in your task manager and protecting your time on your calendar. Both are hard to do if you look at these tools as things to enable you to do more.

Conversely, you could see these tools as enabling you to reduce your workload, for example, by restricting the number of tasks you allow into your task manager daily and weekly. You could also protect certain times of the day for time with your family, exercise, getting outside, and thinking.

If you believe you cannot do any of these things because your boss, clients and colleagues won't let you, you've already lost. The truth is everyone faces this dilemma from time to time. The ones who are more open-minded to testing and changing things are the ones who find ways to get the right work done and protect their time so they can do the things they want to do.

If you want to have more time for what you want to do, start by looking at what you are doing and eliminate the things that don't need to be done. When you begin looking at things from the perspective of "do I need to do this?" you will start to see many things you are doing today that don't need doing. More importantly when you do the daily planning, you are subtracting, not adding.

In the next chapter, we will look at the weekly planning session. This is the time you set aside to look at what you have on your plate and what you have time to get done. It complements the daily planning session because if you have done a good weekly planning session, the daily sessions take a lot less time. However, before we do that, we should look at how we can better prioritize our days.

Prioritizing Your Day

Let's begin with a fact: you have far more tasks to complete than time available. You will never change that unless you are prepared to give up everything – your work, your family, and your friends and live in the middle of a desert. With that fact in mind, you need to find a way to make sure that the tasks you do each day are meaningful, move projects and goals forward, and leave you feeling satisfied at the end of the day.

Prioritization is an art, not a science. This means it is a learned skill. The skill of prioritization is knowing instinctively what is important and what is not and is just something loud and jumping up and down demanding attention. Knowing what your areas of focus are, what they mean to you, and what needs to be done to keep them in balance, you will already have a natural prioritization method. However, we can go a little further.

In the productivity world, there is a prioritization matrix called the Eisenhower Method. This comes from a quote attributed to the former US President, General Dwight Eisenhower:

> *"I have two kinds of problems, the urgent and the important. The urgent are not important, and the important are never urgent."*

To create the Eisenhower Matrix, there are four boxes inside a matrix:

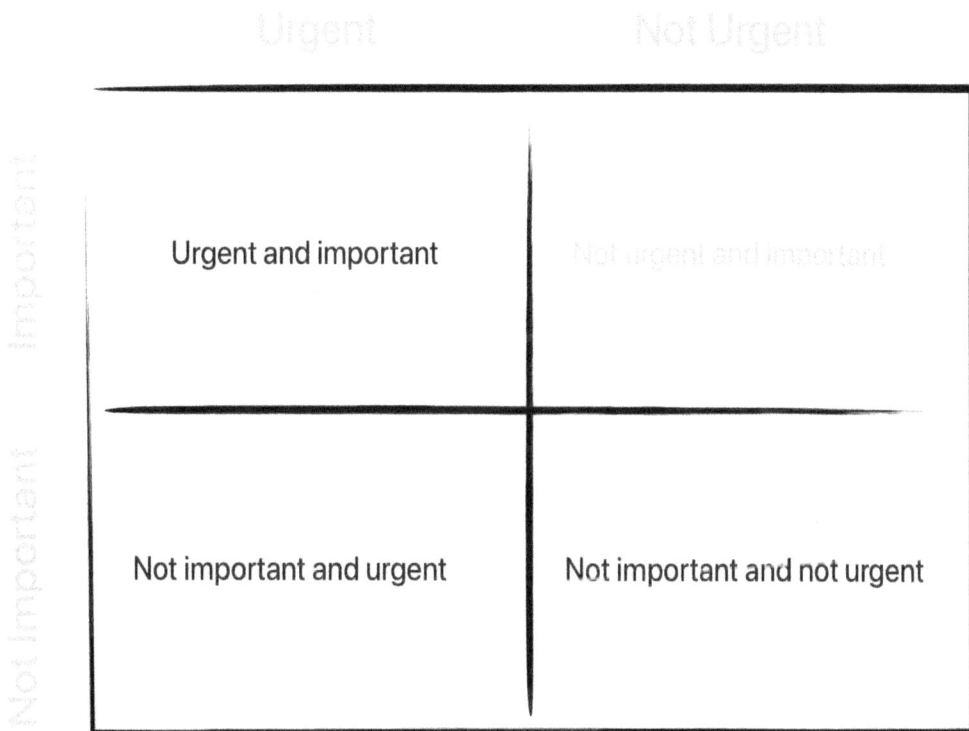

The *important and urgent tasks* are tasks that come from your everyday work. Things like customer or client requests and tasks from your boss, partner, colleagues and other family and friends. The *important and not urgent tasks* are your areas of focus tasks. Exercise, financial well-being, and planning and thinking ahead.

What usually happens when we are not self-aware enough to know the differences between these different sectors is that we spend much of our time in the *important and urgent* and the urgent and not important. This is because, by their nature, these tasks are loudest and are likely to be the urgencies of other people. For instance, if your boss asks you to quickly prepare a record of the sales for your department last month because she has a meeting with her boss later that day, this is not your urgency. It becomes your urgency because your boss asks you for it "urgently," but the real urgency is your boss's.

	Urgent	Not Urgent
Important	Some emails Core work (what you are employed to do) Some meetings Project work Working with your customers	Planning Exercise Working on your goals Self development (education) Rest and relaxation Developing relationships
Not Important	Most emails / slack messages Most meetings Other people's crises Colleague Interruptions Most boss's demands	All social media Online shopping TV Water cooler gossip Searching for new apps

If you have a disorganized boss, over time, you can anticipate their demands and, in some way, prepare for them. For instance, if your boss regularly has a meeting with their boss and you know they will prepare everything at the last minute, you can at least prepare some of the information your boss will ask you for beforehand.

For example, consider a sales report. You could create a spreadsheet to collect the sales data each week and spend a few minutes on a Friday afternoon updating the sheet. This way, when your boss comes asking for it, you have it partially prepared.

This kind of preparedness may seem superfluous and over the top, but what you have done is moved an *urgent and not important* (not important to you) to a *not urgent and important* task (preparation). This is an example of anticipating what could come up and being partially, at least, prepared for it.

However, prioritization begins with your areas of focus.

Prioritization Starts at the Bottom

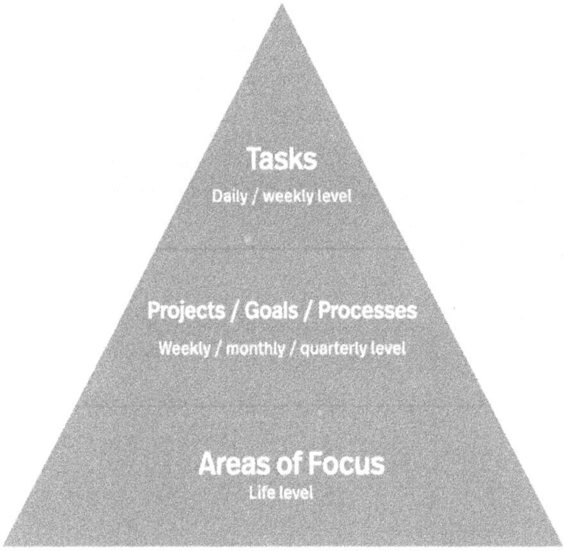
Tasks
Daily / weekly level
Projects / Goals / Processes
Weekly / monthly / quarterly level
Areas of Focus
Life level

- Family and relationships
- Career / business
- Health
- Spirituality
- Personal development
- Lifestyle & Life experiences
- Finances
- Purpose in life.

The starting point of all sustainable productivity systems

The art of prioritization begins at a lower level; this is why you need to know what you want. What do you want to achieve with your career or business? Your social and family life? Your own goals? Being clear about these makes decision-making easier.

Not knowing what you want means everything that comes across your desk is a priority because there is no context to decide. You will revert to basic human needs – the need to please, and the fear of missing out (FOMO), none of which lead you anywhere positive.

For instance, consider your health. No matter where you are with your health, all of us need to make sure we are protecting it. If we are overweight, we should act to reduce our weight. If our diet is a mess and we are eating far too many toxic foods – processed grains and sugar and refined carbohydrates – we should take steps to remove these from our diet. If you are not doing this, you are piling up trouble for yourself later. This would be a *not urgent but important* area. The goal of prioritization is to elevate those important and non-urgent areas to the central part of your task list.

The next step is to make decisions about the work you do. This is likely where your most variable tasks come from.

Why Understanding Your Core Work is Important

When you are called into a meeting by your boss or asked to complete time-consuming sales reports, you are not doing your core work. Teachers completing attendance reports are not doing their core work. Attendance reports help admin staff; they don't help the people you are teaching to learn anything.

In great companies, you don't get promotions or pay raises because you are good at gossiping or fast at replying to messages and emails. You get promoted based on your results doing the work you are employed to do. That is the way it should be, and that is how you are trained to do your work.

Make sure you prioritize the work you were employed to do. Spend a good part of your workday in front of your customers and potential customers, designing products, or teaching and developing teaching materials that will benefit your students. Any work related to these activities should always be your priority.

If you plan your day with these in mind, you will quickly learn where your focus is best applied.

One way to keep your most important tasks front and center is to use your calendar to block sufficient time for them.

If you designate Wednesday night as your date night with your partner, then it will be fixed on your calendar. Your relationship with your partner is important, so schedule time for it. It's a priority – or at least it should be.

Imagine you are a salesperson. Your job is to sell, so you block out perhaps two or three hours each working day to focus on contacting prospective customers and clients (your pipeline). You would also schedule a good part of your day to talk with your existing customers.

That takes care of your core work. However, while doing sales admin and responding to non-sales related emails may not be part of your core work, they are still a part of your job, so you would dedicate a fixed amount of time to dealing with your admin and communications. You will find setting aside an hour or so each day for these tasks will help to keep you on top of them.

Managed well, you would have plenty of time each day for each of these activities while prioritizing the work that drives your core work forward.

Automatic Prioritization

When you are clear about what you want and have defined your core work activities, prioritizing becomes almost automatic. Any task or activity that does not directly support either of those will not be a priority.

Your weekly and daily planning sessions bring all this together. During these sessions, you review your tasks and commitments and decide where best to apply your time. Again, you base these decisions on how any of these requests or activities will assist you with your goals and core work.

Prioritizing is not a science, and you will get better the more you practice it. Knowing what you want, what you are employed to do, and being disciplined enough to make sure you spend most of your time working on these activities, will lead you down roads that take you to greater heights with a lot less stress.

What's On Your Mind? Do That

Part of the problem with overwhelming to-do lists is not knowing where to start. Experience will likely have told you that if you want to know the most important task on your list, it's the one that is most on your mind, the task that bothers you the most; your mind keeps returning to it and giving you a little nudge.

There's a reason why tasks like these are on your mind. It could be because you fear a task will take a long time to complete, so you need to start it right away, or there's a feeling something urgent is lurking, and if you don't do something about it, it will blow up in your face.

Our brains are incredible. They evolved to keep us alive, which is why they filter out 90% of what is going on around us. It would be impossible for your brain to process everything your eyes see.

To test this:

1. Look around the room you are in now.
2. Look for anything that is colored blue.
3. Look everywhere: top, bottom, left, and right.
4. Focus all your attention on everything in the room that is the color blue.

Now, close your eyes and find everything in the room that is the color red.

Okay, open your eyes and look for red. How many red items did you find? How many do you see now? Likely a lot more. That's your brain's Reticular Activating System (RAS) doing its job. Filtering out what it thinks is not important.

Our brains and our senses evolved to find danger, and as we are not always conscious of all our senses at any one time, our instincts kick in and start to warn us something is wrong by drawing our attention to anything it sense is not right. This is why you will often find that a task you have written into your task manager stays in your mind. It's your instincts telling you that this task needs doing soon.

You can fight through these if you wish, but if you want a clear mind to focus on your work and be creative, you will find that making a decision about whatever is on your mind will give you greater clarity throughout your day. That decision could be something as simple as deciding what you will do and when you will do it. All you need to do is to make a decision.

What Do You Do About a Long, Overwhelming List?

If you have a long list of tasks and are feeling stressed out and overwhelmed by them, the best thing you can do is stop doing what you are doing and go through the list task by task.

Select the ten tasks that stand out to you. You will find that when you select ten tasks and commit to completing those before doing anything else, you will instantly feel better, be more focused, and a lot less overwhelmed.

Another way of prioritizing is to go by the deadline date. Pick the tasks that are due first. We start to feel stressed because we have a looming deadline, and our brains will be telling us we don't have enough time to complete the task before the deadline.

This is often not the case; our brains are apt to panic if we have not allocated time to complete a task. To overcome this, find the tasks that have a deadline this week, assign those tasks to be done this week and schedule time on your calendar for getting them done.

This only works if you trust your calendar. If you regularly put things on your calendar and then ignore them, you will never trust your calendar, and the power of your calendar diminishes. You have to have one place among your productivity tools you trust. Task managers are hard to trust because while we may be good at getting things into our task manager, your task manager is not a good time manager. All a task manager does is tell you what tasks need doing, not whether you have enough time to do those tasks.

Only your calendar can tell you whether you have enough time. So, if you have something that needs doing and want to get it off your mind, you need to schedule the time for it on your calendar.

So, whenever you feel stressed out and overwhelmed, stop and look at what is on your mind. You will find that once you have dealt with that – whatever it is – you will soon stop feeling stressed out and get back to ensure you are working on the genuinely important things.

11

The Weekly Planning Session

"The truth is, if you're going to go to the moon, sooner or later, you've got to go to the moon. Now, you can hunch around and do little things in Earth orbit and so on and so on, but if you want to go to the moon eventually, then eventually, you've got to go to the moon." – Glynn Lunney, NASA Flight Director.

When I first began my time management and productivity journey, I could never understand why I needed to sit down on a weekend for an hour or two and plan the week ahead. After all, I was collecting, organizing what I collected, and doing the work. I also noticed that almost every week, my plan never happened. I would be derailed by something or another, and then I was just trying to get back on track.

However, I still needed to do the plan. Why? Because the plan gives you a direction. It gives your week a focus, and it also means if something comes up that requires your undivided attention, you are still able to regain your momentum towards accomplishing what you set out to accomplish.

It is not about reviewing – that's regressive and a form of covert procrastination. It is about setting a few objectives for the week, and all you need to do is focus your energies and time towards meeting those objectives, and you will always be moving forward.

The weekly planning session is the glue that brings everything together. It is during your weekly planning that you will move tasks in your Next Week folder into your This Week folder and look at any tasks you planned to do this week but did not complete.

It is during this session that you can look at your projects and goals and decide what needs to happen next so you can plan out your week.

You will not be able to plan out every hour for your week; there are far too many unknowns that will occur during the week. But you do want to be planning out the things that will move your goals and projects forward. It also gives you a chance to look at your projects at a big-picture level, so you have a better understanding of where you are with everything going on in your life.

When is the best time to do a weekly planning session?

Over the years, I have experimented with different times to do a weekly planning session. From Sunday afternoon to Sunday evening. I've even tried Friday afternoons. None of these times ever felt right. I wondered why this was the case, and in the end, I realized that the timing of your weekly planning session is very important.

Doing it on a Friday afternoon is not great because you are likely to be tired and you will be distracted by other people. Doing it Sunday can leave you feeling demotivated, and often, many of the things on your mind have been forgotten. This is one of the most important tasks you do each week, and not being in the right frame of mind when you do it will guarantee you are not going to do it effectively.

In the end, I found the best time for me to do a weekly planning session is Saturday morning, and there are a number of good reasons for this.

The first is the week is still fresh in your mind so, any issues you were having at work that need a solution are easily recalled. Another reason is you are fresh from a good night's sleep. Most people don't have to wake up early on a Saturday morning, and of all the days in the week, I have found Saturday morning is the most relaxing. And finally, you get your week planned and your mind cleared so you can relax and enjoy the rest of the weekend without worrying about what the week ahead has in store for you.

A weekly planning session does not take very long with the Time Sector System. All you are deciding is what you want to accomplish next week. You do not need to be worrying about the week after or next month. There may be a few projects or events you need to keep an eye on, but all you are doing in a weekly planning session is just that. You are planning out the week.

I have a confession to make: despite what many may think, I rarely complete all my tasks each day, and I often have to reschedule some of my core work time blocks.

I can further confess I don't care. Because one day does not make a week, and I plan for the week rather than the day.

You are a human being, and that means you are going to have great days and some pretty poor days, productively. There's nothing wrong with that; it's just part of being human. There are so many possible ways our energy levels and focus can be disrupted that it would be unreasonable to expect yourself to perform at the highest levels each day.

If you try to push through on days when you feel tired, you will feel tired again the next day. Instead, on those tired days, look at what needs to be done – your must-dos – and your calendar for your appointments, and move everything else off to another day. You can then have a nap or do some chores around the house.

There's no point in pushing through. It's not healthy, and it leads to mistakes that will need to be rectified another day.

The advantage of thinking in terms of what has to be accomplished in a week means on those days when you feel full of energy and "in the zone," you can push through a little and do some of tomorrow's tasks. This works especially well if you can do it on a Monday or Tuesday because you front-load the week, leaving you with less to do towards the end of the week.

Equally, on days when you don't feel great, you don't need to feel anxious because you know you have other days when you can catch up.

Imagine you have an important project due to be completed at the end of next month. You may want to take a look at it to make sure everything is on track. If you discover you have fallen behind and you need to do some work on it to get it back on track, you decide what needs to be done and add that task to your This Week folder.

If, on the other hand, you see there is nothing that needs doing, you can leave it alone. However, as you are going through the project, if you feel it would be important to have a meeting with the key people at the end of the month, you can add that task to your This Month folder. You don't need to date the task at this point because you won't know how busy you will be in the week you want to do it.

If you know it can be difficult to get all the key people together for a meeting, you may decide the best time to arrange a meeting is three to four weeks before; you would then add the task to your This Week folder, date it, and it's done.

When doing a weekly planning session, your focus is on what you want to get accomplished next week. All the other times are irrelevant because you have no idea what will be happening in two or three weeks' time. You may know you will be traveling to Osaka for a conference in three weeks' time, but you won't know for sure what issues you will need to deal with or the number of "urgent" emails you will need to respond to. Things can change so fast; spending time planning out a whole month would be wasted time.

That does not mean you don't plan your month, quarter, or year; what it does mean is your micro-tasks are not planned. You may know what projects you are working on this month and quarter, but what you don't know is what needs to happen next week to move these projects forward.

Here's a quick tip: for projects that involve a lot of consistent work, add the task as a daily or every-other-day task into your task manager and set it to recur as frequently as necessary. This book project has a recurring task each day that says: "Continue writing *Your Time, Your Way* book."

So, what do you look at when you do a weekly planning session? Here's a checklist you may want to use:

- Clear task manager's inbox.

- Review calendar for appointments and commitments for next week.

- Review master projects list.

- Review This Week folder for tasks not completed (why were they not completed?).

- Review Next Week folder, and move tasks for next week into This Week's folder and date the tasks.

- Review This Month folder and move any relevant tasks to This Week.

These tasks are the very basic tasks you would perform every week. However, once a month, there will be some additional areas to review:

- Review goals.

- Review all projects.

- Review calendar for the month.

On a week-to-week basis, you will not need to review all your projects, only your current, active projects. But, at the end of the month, reviewing all your projects – certainly the ones you are working on this quarter – helps you to see far enough ahead to ensure there are no surprises coming your way.

The same applies to your goals. It's easy to lose sight of what you are trying to achieve from your goals when you are doing your daily work and dealing with all the mini-crises that inevitably come up throughout your day and week. Giving yourself a little time each month to go through your goals and evaluate your progress gives you an opportunity to decide if anything needs more attention or refocusing.

On a normal week, your weekly planning should only take you around twenty to thirty minutes. It may take a little longer at first because you are learning a new way of doing things and will be looking at everything. Over time, you will learn what to look at and what you do not need to review. If you remain consistent and do your weekly planning every week, you will quickly learn where you need to look and where you don't need to look. This will speed up the process.

Key Questions to Ask Yourself

Answering a few simple questions helps to keep you focused on what's important:

- What do I want to accomplish this week?

- What must be done?

- What do I want to make significant progress on?

These three questions are powerful. They focus your mind on what's important and ensure what you are scheduling for next week means something to you. Asking, "What must be done?" is the question that should surface up anything you have committed to, and there is a deadline. This could be work for your boss or clients. If you are a student, this could be an assignment that needs to be submitted, or a parent where you need to complete a school application.

What About Tasks You Did Not Complete?

There will be a reason why you were unable to complete a task you had scheduled to be done, and it's good practice to figure out why. It could be you were relying on another person to complete their end of the task, and they did not complete it. Or it could be something else, more important, came up in the day. In these cases, all you need to do is reschedule the task for another day.

Then there are those tasks you added, hoping you would do them, but you knew you were not motivated to do them, so it was always going to be wishful thinking. With these tasks, ask yourself why you are not motivated to do them.

Be honest with yourself here.

Wishfully adding tasks to your This Week folder is demoralizing. If you know you are unlikely to complete a task, do not put it in your This Week folder. Either keep it in your project or goal's note file or keep it in your Next Week folder. You will look at this folder every week, so it is not lost.

The only tasks in your This Week folder should be tasks you intend to do, and if you don't do them, there must be a very good reason for not doing them. Wishful tasks diminish the power of your This Week folder, and its integrity is compromised. If you are not sure when you will do a task, then you can move it off to Next Week and decide when you will do it in your next weekly planning session.

Your Optimal Weekly Task Number

Over time, you are going to learn how many tasks you can reasonably complete each week. If you begin the week with sixty tasks in your This Week folder and at the end of the week, you have twenty tasks remaining, your optimum number is likely to be around forty tasks. Continually having sixty tasks and failing to complete less than 60% of them means you're trying to do more than you are capable of. It's another example of wishful thinking, and it will compromise the effectiveness of your system.

This number is going to be a work in progress. It's likely you will always have incomplete tasks at the end of each week. Three or four of these are not really a problem. It becomes a problem if these are the same tasks you're not getting done each week. In that case, you need to stop and ask yourself why you are not doing them.

> Don't include routine tasks in your optimum number. Routine tasks are not high-priority tasks, and it's seldom a problem if you skip them from time to time.

Your Weekly Planning Session Environment

How consistent would you be with your weekly planning if you always looked forward to doing it? The weekly planning session should be a highlight of your week. It gives you time to reset, adjust and set the tone for the week ahead. It should never leave you feeling anxious or overwhelmed. If anything, it should do the reverse – leaving you feeling what you have planned for next week is meaningful, will move the important things in your life forward, and allow you to reflect on where you are going.

It helps to make the environment pleasant, perhaps by making a cup of your favorite beverage, putting on some of your favorite music, and going to a quiet room to give your planning your full attention. This is something you want to look forward to, and making the environment in which you perform your weekly planning session comfortable and pleasant is going to go a long way toward achieving that.

The weekly planning session brings everything together and makes the Time Sector System so effective. You only need to be concerned about next week. Just seven days. But that only works if you are consistently doing a weekly planning session. If you are not, then you fall into the trap of everything being important, and you will only be working on the latest and loudest tasks. You'll lose sight of your goals and areas of focus, and worst of all, you will lose trust in your system.

The Weekly Planning Matrix

Knowing what needs your attention each week is how you can stay ahead of any issues and avoid building up an impossibly large backlog.

Yet hardly anybody does this. It's as if all they want to do is survive the week with as few dramas as possible, and if they do get to the end of the week without too many mistakes, they feel relieved and repeat the process the following week. Sound familiar?

Your weekly planning session should not be daunting. It's your chance to clear your head, reset and refocus your attention to ensure that where you put your energies each week is in the right place, so the right projects are moving forward, and you are taking care of the things that are important to you.

To encourage you to spend a little time planning the week, I came up with a simple matrix I share with my coaching clients. You can use it to help refocus your attention on what matters to you.

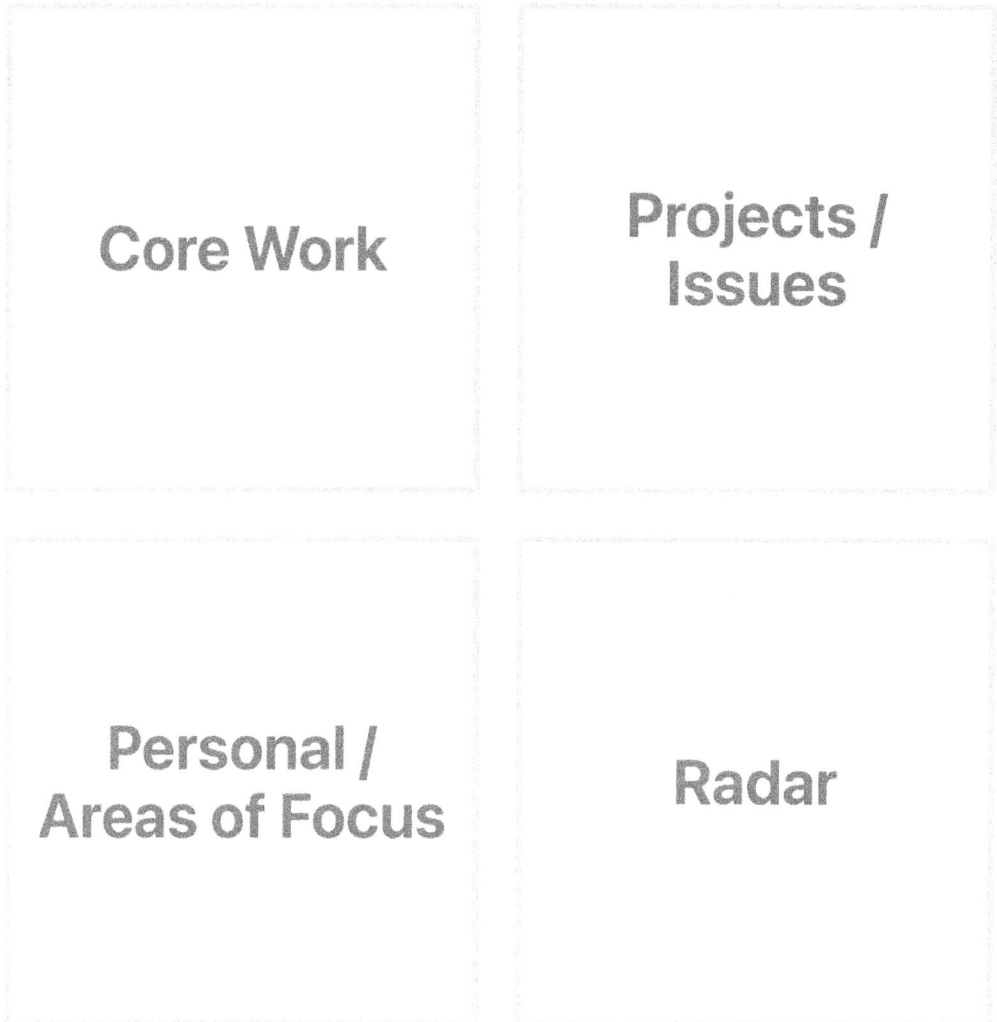

Core Work	**Projects / Issues**
Personal / Areas of Focus	**Radar**

The matrix – what I call "The Weekly Planning Matrix," is a simple four-grid system that covers the most critical parts of your day-to-day life.

- **Core Work** – Your core work tasks sit in the top left box and don't change on a week-to-week basis.

- **Projects / Issues** – What professional projects or issues need your attention next week? You are only looking at the next seven days, so you only include the ones that require your attention next week.

- **Personal** – This quadrant is about your personal areas of focus and any personal tasks/projects you need to take care of next week. This could be arranging your next holiday, meeting with friends, or something as simple as washing your car or cleaning up your garden. Again, this is only looking ahead seven days; it gives you a chance to address any areas of focus you may have neglected, or perhaps get some outstanding errands done.

- **Your Radar** – The final quadrant is your radar. This is for anything you need to keep an eye on or review, as it may be something coming up in the near future. For instance, there may be a project your colleagues are working on that you have oversight on. You may not have anything particular to do on the project, but as you wait for your colleagues to do their bit, you want to keep an eye on it.

Three of the four quadrants will change each week; only your core work will be fixed. Having your core work tasks written out and in the top left of the quadrant means that the first thing you need to do each planning session is to ensure you have sufficient time on your calendar to complete your core work. Your core work is non-negotiable. It must be done.

(Quick tip: to ensure you look at this weekly planning matrix each day, cross off the tasks you have done from the list.)

The best way to do this is to get a sheet of paper and draw out the four squares as above. Then, before opening your calendar or task manager, give yourself ten minutes to think about what needs to be done next week in these four areas. Once you cannot think of anything else, open your calendar and task manager and compare them with your sheet of paper.

In the personal box you can write out any areas of your life you feel need attention. Maybe you need to get to grips with your sleep, or perhaps you have been spending a little too much time on social media and feel you would get greater benefits reading a book or learning to make leather wallets.

Overall, this matrix gives you a simple place to look at each day to ensure your attention is focused on what requires attention.

The key to making this work is always to remember this matrix only concerns the week you are in. Next week is not relevant right now! With that mindset, staying on track and avoiding being distracted by the latest, shiniest object (or productivity app) is far easier.

Extraordinary Planning Sessions

There will be occasions when everything feels out of control. When things are flying at you from all over the place, your stress levels and sense of overwhelm are off the charts. This is when stopping for thirty minutes, turning on your favorite music and sitting down with your system to do a planning session can be advantageous. This will realign you with what you are trying to accomplish. Unfortunately it will also go against every instinct in your body – when we are overwhelmed, our instinct is to work harder, put in more hours, and cram in more work. Yet, often, the best thing you could do is to step back for fifteen or twenty minutes and look at what you have to do and reprioritize.

The number one reason someone comes to me for help is because they feel stressed out and overwhelmed by everything they have to do. They have thousands of emails sitting in their inbox, hundreds of Slack or Teams messages asking for things and a long list of to-dos that never seems to shrink. It's enough to make anyone scream out in sheer desperation. Really, all it takes is thirty minutes to go through everything – not in minute detail, more of an overview – and decide on what the very next thing you need to do, then do it.

The good news is it's possible to regain control. The bad news is you will need to stop and step back a little. It's that stopping and stepping back that people find most difficult.

When you face an impossible situation, the temptation is to keep digging. The problem is what got into the situation you are trying to dig your way out of is precisely what you are continuing to do – digging!

Stop digging, so you can look up and see what you are trying to accomplish, and restart with a clearer direction. That's when, despite all your instincts telling you to keep digging, you must stop and step back.

Then there are those occasions when you return from a vacation or a business trip and have collected a lot of stuff that needs processing. In these situations, giving yourself a little time to complete a planning session will get you back on track and in control.

> If you are going away on vacation, a quick tip here is to avoid using the default email autoreply saying you are away and will deal with email when you return. Don't do that!
>
> Instead, write something along the lines that you are going to be away, and you will be deleting all of your emails. Ask the sender to either contact a colleague or resend the mail when you return. Don't worry; no one will be offended, and you will be able to deal with your mail instantly by selecting all your mail and deleting it. I bet very few of you will have the courage to do it, but I urge you to give it a go.

Your weekly planning session is about giving you a solid base from which to tackle the week ahead, but it can also be used midweek if you find yourself feeling out of control. As the purpose of the session is to give you a foundation, it can also bring everything back to normal and calm your anxious mind.

An Important Warning

Some of the biggest blocks to getting things done are *planning, thinking,* and *preparing.* Unfortunately, none of these get the result you want and are forms of procrastination disguising themselves as doing something important.

Thinking, planning, and preparing do have their place, but they play a very minor role in getting the result you want.

Have you noticed that the biggest reason many people never achieve their goals is not because of a lack of ability or time, but rather a lack of *action*. It's as if people are waiting for the perfect moment to get started with something.

Take starting a podcast. There is nothing complicated in beginning a podcast. All you need is an idea, a microphone, and a computer. Once you have those items in place, start recording. Your first efforts will always be challenging, no matter how much planning and preparation you do. So, just get started. The hardest part of creating a podcast is getting comfortable recording your voice and listening back to yourself speaking.

Once you have a few episodes recorded, you can look at where you will host the podcast and how you will promote it. Hosting and promoting can be done alongside recording. Recording a few episodes first makes it much easier to choose a host for your podcast because you know so much more about what your podcast would sound like.

Creating a productivity system is another example of people overthinking and overplanning. The only questions you need to ask are where will I collect my ideas, commitments, and appointments? How will I organize them? When am I going to do something about them?

Spending months looking at and testing productivity apps is a waste of time. Instead, start with the built-in apps on your phone and computer, and as your system grows, you can look for more elaborate applications if you must.

The great thing about just starting in this way is that you gain so much more practical information about how you collect and organize, and this information can help you make better choices about the kind of tools for you.

Writing a book requires words. How you get those words down doesn't matter. Microsoft Word, Apple Notes, or Google Docs will do all that. You do not need to spend weeks researching and writing applications. Just start writing.

All these reasons for not doing something are excuses. We have access to technology today that our parents' generation could only dream about, and in most instances, the technology is free. You can use Google Docs, Apple Notes, or Microsoft OneNote for free. Our phones have built-in microphones and video cameras. There is no excuse for not doing whatever you want to do.

If you are stalling to begin something, rather than doing more research and planning, stop and ask yourself what's the real reason you are not doing it. Are you afraid of failure? Well, failure is just part of the process of finding success. You need to fail sometimes to learn what doesn't work and change things so that you can succeed.

How many people do you know who have told you they want to start their own business and, several years later, have still not started a business? Starting a business is easy. You create something, and you sell it. Yet, the people who never seem to start their business are wasting so much time writing business plans, deciding what software to use, and designing their logos.

None of that is important if you don't have something to sell. If you have no sales, you have no business. Business plans, logos, and software are not essential until you have customers and something those customers can buy.

Whatever you want to build or create, do whatever it takes to build or make it. The process of doing will inform you what needs to happen next.

Think about all the things you want to do and ask yourself what's stopping you from doing them. If you intend to start your own business, begin a podcast, create online courses, or write a book, find the one step you could take that would contribute directly to having something tangible to show for your idea and do that. The data you get from doing something *real* will inform you of the next step.

12

Using Time Sectors
Every Day

"Sitting still and wishing Makes no person great. The good Lord sends the fishing. But you must dig the bait." – Ian Fleming, Author and Creator of James Bond

Over the last few chapters, we have focused on setting up a system that will work for you. If you have followed along, your goals, areas of focus, and core work are all in either your notes or task manager, and the tasks associated with these are set to recur when they need to recur. The next step is to ask how the Time Sector System will support you throughout the day.

Let's Look at How a "Typical" Day Might Go

You start the day knowing exactly what you are going to work on because you spent ten minutes the evening before making a plan for the day in your daily planning session.

You know what your objectives for the day are (your two must-do tasks), and you made a mental note about what you will be starting the day with.

You are unlikely to need to refer to your task manager first thing in the morning. However, you may need it open, so you are ready to collect anything that comes your way.

For some people, having a review of the plan as part of their morning routines can be helpful and reassuring, particularly for those who get a lot of work through the night. This is a common issue for those who work across multiple time zones. For instance, when it is 10 pm in Tokyo, it is 9 am in New York. So, a colleague in Tokyo is going to bed as you would be starting your day if you were in New York and vice versa. Something could come through via a Slack message or email during the night that needs your urgent attention when you begin the day.

As you are working through the day, you are collecting tasks. For instance, an email you receive from your colleague, Sherry, in Singapore may ask you to review a document. You would add a task "review this document for Sherry" in your task manager's inbox. Likewise, you may be working on a project, and as you are preparing some slides for your presentation, you realize you need to message Ryan in your Houston office about a set of figures you need for the presentation. Rather than stopping what you are doing right now, you can quickly add the task to your inbox.

As you are making coffee, you may remember you need to find out when your daughter's swimming class finishes on Thursday, so you add that task to your inbox.

When you sit back down to do your work with your cup of coffee, you remember you need to put in a holiday request form. Again, you would add this to your inbox.

So, now you have four tasks in your inbox:

- Review this document for Sherry.
- Message Ryan about Texas sales figures from Q2.
- Ask Nicola when her swimming class finishes on Thursday.
- Submit holiday request form to HR for September's holiday.

Notice how these tasks are written. They are clear and tell you immediately what needs to be done. Had you written something like: Document for Sherry" or "Message Ryan," if a crisis occurred or something urgent came up later in the day, before you processed your inbox, it's possible you would forget what the task meant or have to waste time reminding yourself what needed to be done.

156

Be very clear when you write out a task. It might take you a few extra seconds to add more words, but those extra few seconds prevent any mistakes and confusion.

Processing Your Day

As part of your closing down for the day, you would process your inbox. Let's go back to our four tasks.

- Review this document for Sherry.

- Message Ryan about Texas sales figures from Q2.

- Ask Nicola when her swimming class finishes on Thursday.

- Submit holiday request form to HR for September holiday.

Processing begins from the top. So, "review this document for Sherry;" the task itself is clear about what needs doing, and if you have saved the document in a cloud storage site, you may have the link to click on it directly. The only thing you are likely to need to know is how big the document is. If it is a two-page document, you may decide to do that before you finish. After all, it probably won't take you more than ten minutes to do. So you would likely complete that from the inbox. No need to put the task anywhere. If the document was a 30-page article for a medical journal, you probably need an hour or more to review the article. In this case, the question to ask yourself is, when am I going to do it? You look at your calendar and see Thursday afternoon looks reasonably free, so you can add it to your "This Week" folder and date it for Thursday.

It's likely at this stage, you will not need to block the time required on your calendar, but if Sherry needs this reviewed before the end of the week, you may decide to block the time out.

Next one: "Message Ryan about Texas sales figures from Q2." Now, in this case, Ryan could be on holiday until next week, so you can just drag this task straight to your Next Week folder. There's nothing you can do about it this week, so push it off to next week.

"Ask Nicola when her swimming class finishes on Thursday." This is another task you can do today; you will likely complete it from the inbox. So, there's nothing to do there.

Finally, "Submit holiday request form for September holiday." This could be something you need more information about before you can do it. For instance, you may need to confirm with your partner when they want to take the holiday and confirm your hotel reservation. So, this task will depend on when it needs to be done. For instance, if you don't need to do it until later in the month, you could add the task to your "This Month" folder.

However, with this task, you have identified you need to talk to your partner and make a hotel reservation. So you would add a task "Talk to Michael about when he wants to take our September holiday." At this stage, you don't need a task for making the hotel reservation. You don't know who will do it. Michael may say he will do it.

Michael could be away on a business trip right now, so in this case, you would add the new task to your This Week folder and date the task for Saturday. The original task of submitting your holiday request form can then be moved into your This Month folder. This way, you are not going to miss it. It will come up when you next do a weekly planning session.

In the time you have read these few words, you will have processed four tasks from your inbox. It will have taken you longer to read this passage than it would to process those four tasks.

Over time, you will get faster at doing this. It will become almost second nature. The process is:

What is it? What do I have to do? When am I going to do it? And that's it. When you process your inbox, and ask those three questions, you will be following a solid sequence of steps, and with consistency and practice, you will inevitably get faster.

There will be tasks that come up while you are working on a project or in a meeting about that project. These are best going straight into your project note. They need thinking through, and there's a chance that some of those tasks may not need to be done at all. Watch out for tasks involving researching or reading something. These types of tasks end up being ignored when in your task manager. Instead, add them to your project note. You'll eventually get to a point in the project when, in order to proceed, you will need to do the research or the information you need is given to you through another source, so you no longer need to do the research.

However, when you are working on your projects, be aware of any tasks that need to be done at specific times. For instance, as you are working on a project, you may notice that two or three tasks need to be done this week. Move these tasks to your task manager. You may not need to go back into the project note that week, so you want to see these when they come up. Likewise, if you are certain a task will need to be done next week, take that task and add it to your Next Week folder. For conditional tasks – tasks that cannot be done until something else has been completed first – leave these in your project note. There are probably too many unknowns at this stage, and you may find the task no longer needs to be completed.

For most projects, you will be working on these individually. What I suggest you do is create tasks such as "continue working on project X" or "review project Y" and then move to your project notes. After all, that is where all your relevant information will be held.

It's likely you will also get a lot of incoming tasks throughout the day that need to be dealt with immediately. With these, you can either do them immediately – bypassing your inbox – or add them to your inbox for doing later in the day. When you do these will be dependent on what you are doing at the time the task comes in.

Because there are so many unknowns that will happen throughout your day and the likelihood that something you thought would take thirty minutes takes two hours, it's important to avoid overloading your daily task list. I know it's very tempting to load it up and believe you will have time to get everything done, but the reality is it's unlikely you will. Always err on the side of less, not more.

The great thing about focusing on elimination rather than accumulation is if you do manage to get everything done early, you always have the option to look at what you can do from your list of things to do tomorrow. (Or take a rest and enjoy the day – the best option).

What About Email?

We will cover this in more detail in the chapter on email, but actionable emails should not be in your task manager. For many of you, many of your tasks will come from email, and it can be very tempting to throw the whole email into your task manager. Many current task managers have add-ons or plug-ins to add your task manager to your email app, which makes it even easier to add actionable emails to your task managers.

If there are far too many of these emails that require action, and you are sending them to your task manager, they quickly fill up your inbox to a point where it becomes overwhelming. Add to this that every time you go to respond to the email, you are switching between apps (your task manager to your email app and back again). This becomes a very inefficient way to manage these emails.

Instead, create a folder in your email to manage these emails. Then, at a given time each day, you work on clearing this folder.

The goal is to keep your task manager as clean and tight as you can. Throwing actionable emails in there adds more and more stuff to your task manager when it is easier to keep all this in one place -- your email app – and have a single task that reminds you to clear that actionable folder each day.

Random Tasks

These are tasks that are not connected to a project or a goal that just need doing. You could receive a message to drop by your HR office to pick up some papers, or you're asked to call someone about a request you made. For these, drop them in your inbox if you cannot do them right now. If you do have time to do them at the time you receive them, then just do them.

The Daily and Weekly Planning Connection

Once you've processed your inbox, the next step is to plan your day tomorrow.

When daily planning, look at your calendar. This is important because events will have been added to your calendar as your week progresses; you will want to be reminded of these. It's also likely you may have added a meeting to your calendar that slipped your mind. By reviewing your calendar, you get to pick up on these well in advance.

Once you have your calendar reviewed, check your list of tasks for tomorrow. The question here is, *are these still relevant?* It's surprising how often a task you added a week ago is no longer relevant and can be removed from the list. Another possibility is a task you thought you would be able to do can no longer be done because something else came up that has caused a delay or is more important. With these tasks, you can either remove the date and move the task to your Next Week folder or if you know the date and it is later this month, you can add the new date and move the task to your This Month folder. You will see it when you next do a weekly planning session.

That's it. That's how you process your inbox and a daily planning session. Again, it's worth repeating; if you do your daily planning session consistently – and that means every day – you will soon get fast at this, and it becomes something you naturally do.

And that's really what becoming better at managing your time is all about. Turning the mechanics of using your system into something you automatically do because not doing so is something you associate with pain.

Our brains are pulled towards pleasure and pushed away from pain. If you associate doing any of your planning sessions with pain – you feel it's boring, for instance – you will resist. If you associate not doing a planning session with pain (which will be true), you are more likely to do it.

You will enjoy doing the planning sessions because you know the massive benefits you get from doing them. You are much more relaxed, feel more in control and feel a sense of freedom in not having to worry about what you are not doing. Once you know what you are doing and what you are *not* doing, you don't worry because you have time allocated for the things that you want to do later in the week.

The same occurs when you collect everything. Once you trust your system, you find as soon as you have collected something into your system, you immediately feel a sense of relief. You know you will not forget anything. Whether that something is in your notes app or task manager doesn't really matter. If it's in, and you are consistent with the planning sessions, you know you will not miss it, and you can make a decision about it later.

Homework

Before you finish your day today, go through your task manager's inbox and clear it. Ask the three questions: What is it? What do I need to do? When will I do it? Then review your calendar for tomorrow's appointments and make sure you have not been too enthusiastic about what you can do tomorrow.

Time yourself doing these steps. You can use that time as a benchmark for your future planning sessions.

13
Common Pitfalls

I like to refer to this strategy as addition by subtraction. The Japanese companies looked for every point of friction in the manufacturing process and eliminated it. As they subtracted wasted effort, they added customers and revenue. Similarly, when we remove the points of friction that sap our time and energy, we can achieve more with less effort. - James Clear

Over the many years I have been obsessed with time management and productivity systems, I have made most of the mistakes and pitfalls that, if you are new to time management systems, you are likely to make. In this chapter, I will list some of the most common ones so you can avoid them or, at the very least, spot them when they begin to take effect.

Not Collecting Everything

Your brain is incredible, yet it can often feel it is conspiring against you. You are asked to do something when you get home, and the moment you arrive at your front door, you completely forget what it was you were asked to do. You take your glasses off, go and do something, and within a few minutes, you cannot remember where you put your glasses. Your brain is great at recognizing patterns, regulating your core temperature, and telling you when something is wrong, but for a seemingly simple task such as taking the laundry out of the washing machine and hanging out the clothes, it forgets to remind you.

Your brain was not designed to remember numbers or things to do, like hang out the laundry. Your brain evolved to avoid danger and pain and seek pleasure. This is why, when you see an aggressive dog growling at you and baring its teeth, you know to move away. How do you know that? It's your experience, either personal or taught. You recognize the pattern – the aggressive stance, the growl and the baring of teeth. Your instinct is to move away.

Your brain is not working against you; asking it to remember a number or an errand is not what your brain evolved to do. It evolved to remind you to eat by releasing hormones that make you feel hungry, to sleep by releasing melatonin and to crave sugar by releasing dopamine whenever you eat a piece of chocolate. Your non-essential reminders need to be externalized, and the best place to do this is in a to-do list or notes app.

Work with your brain instead of against it and develop the habit of collecting everything. Set up your mobile phone so it is easy to collect anything that might be important: an idea, an errand, or a commitment you have made. Even if you do remember it, having it collected in your system means you will soon begin to trust your system.

Not Trusting Your System

Linked to not collecting everything, if you continue to try and remember things rather than getting them into your system, you will never trust your system. It's an all-or-nothing change that needs to be made. Doing this halfheartedly will mean you will never truly trust you have everything where it needs to be.

When you begin using COD and the Time Sector System, the first objective is to develop the habit of collecting *everything*. That means becoming comfortable writing things down when you are with someone and ensuring you have your "universal collection tool" with you at all times (including the bathroom!)

Once you trust yourself to collect everything that may or may not be important, you will be confident that nothing has been missed, and when you process what you collected (organize), you can decide whether something needs to be done or can be deleted.

Confusing Apps for Systems

Your time management and productivity skills come from the system you practice and *not* the apps you use. Any task manager or digital note-taking app can work with the Time Sector System, as they can with any other productivity or time management system. It's never about the apps you are using.

The danger of promoting an app as a substitute for a system and set of practices you follow is you will be forever switching apps. App switching is a drain on your productivity and is a form of procrastination because every time you change your app, you have to transfer your current data from the app you were using to the new app and then spend weeks and months learning how to use your new app effectively. Most app switchers never give an app enough time to prove its worth before they are off to the next new thing because someone's told them how the latest app is going to be the answer to their productivity woes.

Let me be crystal clear with you here: NO, IT WON'T!

The truth is no new app will *ever* be perfect. If it was, it would never need updating, and most people these days don't like apps that are not updated frequently. Evernote is a great example. Evernote launched around 2007 as a simple note-taking app. It was one of the first notes apps on the App Store and was widely taken up. It quickly became one of the most popular third-party note-taking apps. It made a few mistakes along the way. It added a lot of features that were not part of its core philosophy and even went into merchandising. Then, around 2016, it decided this was not the right direction and removed a lot of features.

However, on the positive side, Evernote was becoming stronger and more reliable throughout this time. Then, towards the end of 2019, it was announced that Evernote needed to be completely refreshed. There would be no new features, and all the developers and engineers would be working on the new Evernote. Then everything went quiet.

It only took a couple of months before people were saying Evernote was finished. It was slow, and there was a lack of development. It's strange how, for an app to be considered "good," it has to be constantly adding new features. The reality is for an app to be good, it needs to be solid, dependable, and fast. *Not* adding new features all the time.

One of the best text editing apps around is an app called BBEdit. BBEdit is currently on its fourteenth edition. Their first edition came out in 1992. That was over thirty years ago! This means that the app updates roughly every two years. You won't find many people on YouTube doing reviews or talking about BBEdit because it's not sexy enough. It's "too old."

Yet, many long-term Mac users still use it [*https://www.macworld.com/article/233511/bbedit-13-review-a-lucky-number-indeed-for-revered-macos-text-editor.html*]. They use it because it is solid and dependable, and when a new edition is launched, it works without changing the character or feel of the app. The developers, Bare Bones Software, are not trying to make BBEdit for the masses; they make a high-quality product for people who know what the best is.

If you are new to productivity and time management software, then you are likely to spend a few weeks and sometimes months experimenting and finding what works best for you. Once you do find an app you like, stick with it. This will ensure you learn how to use the app properly, you'll know how to use keyboard shortcuts, and you will know where to find every menu item.

Tips For Choosing Apps

Here are a few tips that will help you when it comes to selecting the right app:

- *Use apps you like the look of.* If you don't like the way an app looks and feels, you are not going to enjoy using it. As there are thousands of apps on app stores to choose from, you are almost certain to find an app that appeals to your aesthetic preferences.

  - *Go for simpler apps.* Complex apps promise a lot of features – which is what causes them to be complex – and with all those features, once you begin storing a lot of information in them, they may begin to slow down significantly, and you may find you're restarting the app because one feature or another stops working.

  - *Avoid expensive apps.* They are rarely worth the money, and those that are, are designed for large organizations, not necessarily for individuals. With apps, you will often find the ones in the middle price range do the best job.

  - *Look for apps that have been around for a long time.* New apps look great, and they probably spend a lot of money on advertising and marketing. Many of these will fail, and if you have committed to a new app and it disappears or is bought by another company, be prepared for a lot of time transferring your data to another new app.

  - *Start with free apps.* When you start building your system, you will be learning your system. Built-in apps by Apple, Google, and Microsoft are the best ones to begin with because they are free and have a relatively easy learning curve. The last thing you need is to build a system that works for you while trying to learn how to use a more complex app.

Don't Skip the Planning Sessions

Everything works because you are doing your daily and weekly planning sessions consistently. Skipping one occasionally will not have a detrimental effect on your progress, but if you don't do them, period, your whole system will eventually fall apart.

Your daily planning session takes no more than fifteen minutes, and your weekly planning session takes around thirty minutes. If you cannot find those few minutes each week, you should reevaluate your priorities and your discipline.

Skipping the weekly planning session means you are not moving tasks forward to your This Week folder. It also means you don't know where you are in your projects, and that means you'll be working reactively. The whole purpose of the Time Sector System is to move you towards working proactively, to put you in control of what you do and where you spend your time. When you skip the planning sessions, you let time and other people control you, and that never leaves you feeling happy or fulfilled.

In my coaching practice, almost every client who is struggling to get themselves organized and their work done are the ones who are not doing their planning sessions. It's the planning sessions that are the difference between successfully becoming organized and more productive or being in a continuous struggle.

Putting Too Much Into Your Task Manager

This pitfall may seem contradictory to the first two about collecting everything; however, once you have everything collected, you will need time to filter what you collect. If you collect a task such as "read this article" and then just leave it in your system, you will not do it. Other, more important things will inevitably land on top of that task, and eventually, it will disappear somewhere in your system.

The goal with your task manager is to keep it clean and tight, and that means you want to filter what eventually ends up in your system. When you process your inbox, you can ask the question, "Am I going to do this anytime soon?" If the answer is *not really*, or *I'm not sure*, you can add the task to a note in your notes app. Having a list of articles to read, books to read, places to visit, etc., in your notes app is a more natural place for this kind of task, and so your task manager will stay relevant and not be filled with those wishful tasks – the tasks you hope to do one day.

When you are strict about what gets into your task manager and you let your notes app do the heavy lifting, you'll find yourself a lot more focused. When your task manager is full of small, less meaningful tasks, it will soon fill up and become bloated, and you'll stop looking at it because it is overwhelming.

Continually Fiddling and Tweaking

There needs to be time for you to learn and to build habits, so your system works. This means collecting everything, giving yourself a little time each day to organize what you have collected and to do your daily and weekly planning sessions.

While at first you may experiment with when and how you do these things, at some point, you will need to work on your system and give it time to embed itself into your daily life. If you are always fiddling with *how* you do things, you will delay that settling-in period.

What you may find works is to set up a routine task in your routines folder, reminding you to review your system every three months. This way, you have a way to adjust things, and you can keep a note where you can add thoughts and ideas that could be useful when you come to review your system.

Look out for areas that you feel slow you down. For instance, one user found that her weekly planning took two to three hours each week. When she analyzed how she was doing her weekly planning, she realized that she was reading through all her project notes every week. If you are consistent with your weekly planning, this will be something you won't need to do. Not all projects will be active, and some will be moving quicker than others. The only projects you need to look at in your weekly planning are the ones that are going to be active the following week.

One tip you can use here is to use a master projects list to add a date for the next review. That will speed things up considerably.

Mishandling "Waiting For" / "Follow-up" Tasks

This is one of the biggest areas people struggle with. It sounds pretty logical to create a list of all the people you need to follow up with or stuff that you are waiting for. Get it all onto the list, and then you can see it all in one place.

The problem starts when this list becomes very long. And unless you are curating it and dealing with it every day, that is precisely what will happen. Follow-ups and waiting for tasks are rarely urgent tasks. People put them on lists so that they don't forget about them.

If you're waiting for something, there is obviously going to be a trigger somewhere. Imagine you've sent your passport application to the passport office. You have a trip coming up in three months' time, and you're waiting for your new passport to arrive. The trigger is when you're looking at your trip's project; you will see at the top of that list whether you have or have not received your passport. Do you really need to put that on *another* list?

Waiting-for tasks are incomplete tasks. If you need a copy of a report from a colleague and they tell you they will send it to you later, the task is not complete. The task is to get a copy of the report, it's not to wait for Seth to send you the report. Until you have the report, the task is not complete.

For follow-ups generally, this involves reaching out to people; perhaps you've been to a trade fair, and you picked up a lot of people's names and email addresses, and you want to follow up with them. This is a task that needs to go on the calendar. Sure, you will have a list of all the people you want to follow up with, but that would be better managed from a spreadsheet. However, when are you going to do that? That is really the question. You know precisely what you need to do, but the question is when are you going to do it?

For something like this, schedule an hour or two on your calendar and get the list in front of you. Start at the top and work your way down it. That is how you deal with those kinds of tasks.

A waiting-for task is, in effect, an incomplete task related to someone else. If your task is to get a new passport, until you have the passport in your hand, the task is not complete. Sending the passport application to the passport office is just a part of a bigger task which is to get a brand-new passport. so you send off your passport application, and now the task has to be moved forward. If the task is to get a new passport, you would schedule that six weeks into the future, or depending on how long, on average, it takes to get a new passport, and then that will come up on the specified day. The question is, do you have a new passport? If not, then the task is still not complete, and then you need to make a decision on what needs to happen next.

Putting Everything Into Your This Week Folder

If you find yourself putting everything into your This Week folder, that will mean you have created an impossible week. You won't be able to complete everything in there. The tasks you did not complete were all the tasks that did not need doing this week. After all, if they did need doing this week, they would have been done!

For this, the best advice is to review what you did not complete. Is there a pattern or a link? If you are not doing a particular type of task, you want to be asking *why*. What is it about these tasks you feel should be done this week, but you are not doing?

The goal of the Time Sector System is to learn to prioritize and to see patterns. With that experience, you begin to get a better handle on your day and week so that you can plan accordingly.

The same applies to email. If I had to deal with 150+ actionable emails a day, that would require at least two hours each day dedicated to managing those emails. Imagine not responding for one day. That would mean you now have a backlog of 300+ emails. Therefore, I recommend you have a non-negotiable two-hour block dedicated to communication each day. That way, you can stay on top of your mail. Without those two hours, you would be in trouble.

For your customer work, there are going to be some common requests that require immediate action and some that can wait until the next time you speak with them. creating a set of rules for dealing with these will give you a framework to work from.

If you treat each customer request as being urgent (priorities again), you will never gain control over your day.

Not Finishing Personal Projects

Unlike work-related projects, personal projects rarely have any accountability. At work, there's likely to be a boss setting parameters and deadlines, and colleagues who depend on you to do your part. With personal projects, this accountability is likely to be almost nonexistent.

However, before any project can succeed, whether business or personal, there needs to be a clearly defined outcome – a single sentence that states the desired outcome and when it must be completed. One of the most famous project-clarifying sentences was given by John F. Kennedy in 1961 when he said:

> (The US) "should commit itself to achieving the goal, before this decade is out, of landing a man on the Moon and returning him safely to the Earth."

Twenty-six words that set NASA on a course that captivated the world. Those words were clear, contained a deadline, and left no one in any doubt about what was to be achieved.

It did not matter that much of the technology and know-how had not been invented when Kennedy spoke those words. Developing the technology and know-how was for the scientists and engineers to figure out. All that mattered was a clear outcome (desired result) and a timeline.

So, before you begin your project, develop your clarifying sentence – a sentence that clearly states your desired outcome and when you will complete it.

Avoid the mistake many people make at this stage: wasting time thinking and planning. Thinking and planning are the opposite of acting. They are often used as an excuse not to act – what I call "covert procrastination." Once you have a clear outcome, you don't need to spend a lot of time thinking and planning. All you need is the very first action step.

For example, if you were to build a conservatory on the side of your house, the first step would be to get some quotes so you can decide if the project is financially viable. It would be a complete waste of time and energy to spend several months thinking about it if you had yet to learn the projected cost.

Imagine you decide with your partner that you would like to build a conservatory. Then, the next day, you contact some companies that build conservatories to give you a quotation.

You may also need to find out if you require any planning permissions from your local government office, and if so, what forms would you need to complete?

Without this information, nothing is going to happen. This is why taking the first logical steps is essential once you have decided to proceed with the project. The following steps will naturally fall into place.

For instance, once you have the quotations, the next step would be to secure finances. Once that's done, you would hire the right company to go ahead and build it for you.

Smaller projects (or goals) work the same way. Taking a trip to the Grand Canyon, for instance. When will you go, who will you go with, and where will you stay?

Where's the Antagonist?

There is one more part to completing personal projects that is required. You want to have an antagonist. NASA's antagonist during the moon landing program was the Soviet Union. This is why they called it the Space Race: NASA and the Soviet Union were racing to be the first to the moon.

Competitors, rivals, or enemies bring energy to a project. It's that sense of urgency that stops hesitation. For most of us, we will be unlikely to have a natural competitor; however, there is one source where you will always find an antagonist. That is within yourself.

One of the reasons we struggle to complete our projects is because of ourselves. As human beings, we can be naturally lazy. That was a good thing when food was scarce, but we don't live in that world today. For most of us, food is in abundance all year round. We do not need to conserve our energy for hunting food.

That laziness manifests itself in many ways. The soft seduction of our sofas when we know we should be washing up, the enveloping warmth of our beds on a cold winter morning, and the ease of ordering fast food after a hard day's work. These all conspire to prevent us from doing what we know we should be doing.

Whatever your weakness, you identify it and make it your enemy. Decide from now on; you will never let your sofa, bed, or local fast food delivery service win. Whenever you find yourself being seduced by any of these antagonists, stop, say no, and immediately go and do what you know is right.

Once you have decided on your project, written out a clear, clarifying sentence, and identified your antagonist(s), take the first step. Start that diet, call the builders, or buy storage boxes to clear out a room in your home. Just do the first natural task. One thing you must never do is tell yourself you need to do more planning. Planning never gets the job done. The only way you will complete your project is to act.

The Pernicious Procrastination Cycle

Do you have big dreams, things you want to accomplish in your life, goals to achieve, or a lifestyle you want to create? How are you doing in working towards achieving those? If you are like most people, you likely find you don't spend much time on these, yet you have already decided they are important.

One of the biggest reasons for this is procrastination. We think about what we want, begin to give some thought about how we will achieve it and then get pulled away by another blog post on motivation or productivity or a video by Mel Robbins or Robin Sharma. It becomes a never-ending cycle. We sit down with the intention of finally doing something about what we want and get dragged off in directions we had not intended to go.

Most of the time, the reason you never actually start doing these personal projects or goals want to accomplish is you have not clearly defined what it is you actually want. You may have a vague idea – to build a solid financial foundation for your future, for example– but it is only a vague idea, and every time you sit down to develop a plan, you begin to feel overwhelmed, so a Ray Dalio video on investing seems close enough to make you feel like you are doing something.

To avoid this kind of procrastination, get very specific. What do you define as being financially secure? How much money do you need? What investments will you need to make? How will you grow your investments? Unless you answer these specific questions, you will always struggle to get started. The task will always feel too big. The solution is to break things down into bite-sized chunks so you can begin moving forward and build momentum.

Whatever it is you want to achieve, unless you are intentional about doing what you need to do to make it happen, it will never happen. Knowing you should spend more time with your kids is very different from spending time with your kids. As Tony Robbins says, you need to "turn your shoulds into musts." "I should spend more time with my kids" is never going to happen. "I must spend more time with my kids" has a much greater chance of becoming a reality.

To do this, start by using your calendar. Whatever it is you want to change or begin doing, schedule time on your calendar to do it. To make something happen consistently, you need to set a regular time to do the activity. If that is spending time with your kids, get it on your calendar. If you want to master a new language, get your study time on your calendar. If you want to save more money, put sending money into your savings account into your task manager.

Whatever it is you want to do, be *intentional*. Set a day and a time when you will do what needs to be done and stick to it. You don't accidentally roll out of bed at 5 AM in the morning and go out for a run. You go out running when you intend to wake up early and go out running.

Procrastination can also be caused by the way you write your tasks. As we saw earlier, If you do not make it clear what you intend to do when you write a task and instead write something like "next week's presentation," when you see a task like that, it's immediately unclear what needs to be done. Instead, write the task with an action verb. For example, "Prepare slides for next week's presentation" or "Get figures for next week's presentation." Writing tasks in this way ensures you know precisely what needs to be done.

Consistency is a key component of any person's success. Without consistency, nothing will change. Saving $100 in January and then not saving anything else until July is not going to give you the results you want. Likewise, if your goal is to wake up early and you only get up early once a week, you are not achieving anything.

When you consistently schedule your activities on your calendar, when the time comes to do whatever you need to do, you don't need to think about what to do next; you will know exactly what you need to do, and you will do it.

Being aware of what you do when you procrastinate helps you to stop yourself from doing it. If you find yourself aimlessly scrolling through Instagram, don't let yourself go near Instagram until you have completed the task you want to complete. In extreme cases, delete the app from your phone. Although this is not necessary, if you cannot resist the urge, delete it. Alternatively, hide it on a screen you rarely go to so the temptation is not there.

Knowing what your procrastination habits are goes a long way to helping you avoid situations where you are likely to procrastinate.

Discipline, along with consistency, are two of the most powerful traits of highly successful people. Without discipline, you will never get yourself out exercising or sitting down to study applied economics. You need discipline, and the good news about discipline is it is like a muscle. The more you exercise it, the stronger it becomes.

To develop your discipline, all you need to do is start small. Begin by limiting your social media time to lunchtimes and evenings for thirty minutes, for example. Learn how to say "no" to yourself. When you find yourself procrastinating, say "no" to yourself and stop doing whatever it is you were procrastinating with. Go for a short walk or get up off the sofa and do the dishes. Do something other than what it was you were procrastinating with.

Over time, you will find yourself being stronger mentally, and that will set you up to be much better at preventing yourself from procrastinating.

Procrastination is not all bad. There are times when your brain needs a distraction to be creative. Procrastination is bad when it stops you from doing your important work or does not allow you to get on with achieving your goals. When that happens, you want to take steps to stop yourself. Be specific about what you want to achieve, be intentional with your time consistently and be aware of your procrastination triggers. These habits will allow you to develop the necessary discipline to be more focused on what you want and will take you further towards achieving the success you are capable of.

However, there is often another reason why you procrastinate. That is because you are mentally tired. Being unable to focus, and getting distracted, is a sign your brain needs a break. It could be a short twenty-minute walk outside is enough for you to give your brain a rest. Sometimes, though, you may need to stop for the day and take a rest.

If you push through on days you feel tired, you won't get much done, and what you do will probably be filled with errors. It also means the next day is rarely any better. If you stop for the day, take a rest, or do some physical activity, the next day is far better. You can get a lot more done.

In these situations, do the essentials and leave the rest until later in the week. It means rather than having two or three days where you struggle to get work done; you only have half a bad day.

14

How to Get Focused Each Day

"Wake up early and tackle the day before it tackles you.
Be on offense, not defense." – Evan Carmichael

One of the most effective ways to create a more balanced, productive life is to create a structure within your daily life. If you have no structure, you are pushed and pulled all over the place and will inevitably end up on someone else's agenda. This is never a good place to find yourself. It's when you are pushed and pulled by the events around you – your boss's demands, requests for help from friends and family, and allowing yourself to become angry because of what you read online; you will achieve nothing.

One way to do this is to begin and end your day with a set of routines. These do not need to be very complex; all they need to do is give you time for yourself and get you focused on the day ahead. It's a far better way to begin your day than being triggered by the latest outrage on social media or in the news.

If you want to take control of your life, you will need some structure and routine in it. Having a structured, routine life doesn't mean you lose your freedom. Rather, you lose your freedom by not having a structure or a routine, because you will always end up working for other people's benefit. Sure, you have the perceived freedom to go out with your friends at any time, but that means you are now tied to your friend's agendas, not yours. Where's the freedom in that?

To begin building empowering routines in your life start with your mornings. The chances are you are already following a morning routine. You wake up, get out of bed, go to the bathroom, brush your teeth, make coffee, etc. Whatever you currently do in the morning, it will be something you likely do every morning, whether it is intentional or not. So, to begin a routine in the morning, start with what you would like to do.

Things like:

- Meditate.
- Exercise.
- Journal.
- Learn.
- Read.
- Write daily pages.

You will find that by adopting some of these into a morning routine, you will start to develop some very positive new habits. You are training that all-important self-discipline.

The key to creating a morning routine you follow is you do what you *want* to do. Perhaps you've watched videos or read about what other people do in their morning routines, and you felt inspired. The problem is that those routines work for the person doing them. They do not necessarily work for you. Many people begin their day by doing exercise at 6:00 am in the morning. This works for them, but you may not be a morning person. If you try to exercise that early in the day, you may come to hate it and eventually, you will stop. That's not the purpose of developing a set of empowering morning routines.

Your morning routines need to empower you, set your day up right, and leave you feeling ready for the day ahead.

> Author Robin Sharma developed a structured morning routine called the 5 AM Club. His routine starts when he wakes up at 5 AM and begins with 20 minutes of sweaty exercise. After that, he plans his day for 20 minutes. Then, he finishes the hour with 20 minutes of learning.

I tried this routine several years ago for around eighteen months. It was lovely waking up at 5 AM; it was quiet, and I got very focused. The problem I had with it was that I am not naturally a morning person, and I was working late into the evening. This meant I was not getting enough sleep.

This meant I needed to adjust something, and I realized that was the time I woke up. When you think about it, the power of a morning routine like the 5 AM Club is not the *time* you wake up; it's what you *do when* you wake up.

Your evening routines are for closing out the day. They help prepare you for a good night's sleep.

The key to a good set of evening routines is that they relax you. Doing things like reading, writing in your journal, meditating, or going for an evening walk. You can also use this time to review your plan for tomorrow. This puts your mind at rest, so you reduce the chances of becoming anxious that you may have missed something.

If you are new to these routines, I would suggest you create a checklist in your notes app for them. This way, you can keep a record of how successful you are at performing them. The goal is to do them consistently, and having a checklist not only helps you to remember what to do but it also helps you to develop the right habits.

Both your morning and evening routines are there to empower you. To give you time to reflect and, more importantly, give you time for yourself. Just a few minutes each day when you have some time dedicated to your needs will enhance your mental health, give you time to think about what you want and ensure that what you are doing each day is taking you in the right direction. This time alone will give you an edge in life.

How To Start Your Day Motivated and Energized

I once was asked why a person would start the day with dread and a lack of enthusiasm. I remember I also had those feelings. It was a strange place to be, and I realized a lot was down to me and how I looked at the work I was doing.

If you think about it, the way the media (and social media in particular) portrays work is that it's a necessary evil. It stops you from doing what you want to do and can destroy relationships. Yet, we never think of formal education in this way. We encourage our kids to work hard at school, study hard in the evening, pass exams, and go off to university, building up giant debts before they even begin their professional lives.

Work is an extension of your education. You have likely learned more from your career than you ever learned at school or university. School and university teach you the theory; your work teaches you practical skills.

School does not necessarily teach you how to sell, negotiate, manage your time and finances, or to write a proposal. You will learn these practical skills when you join the workforce.

When you stop thinking of your work as a necessary evil and instead see it as an education, you start to see the possibilities ahead of you. Each day, you get to learn; you have opportunities to fail, make mistakes, and learn from them and from other people. You gain experience, and that experience will stay with you forever.

Other areas will guarantee you have an energetic day; I know how tempting it is to sit up late at night watching TV or scrolling through social media. It feels restful and relaxing, yet it is destroying your sleep time. Certainly, watch TV and scroll your social feeds, but give yourself a cutoff time.

Perhaps after you finish a work session or a meeting, do some activity for ten minutes or so. Go to the bathroom, walk up a few flights of stairs, or, if you work from home, do some chores such as taking the laundry to your washing machine or washing dishes – anything involving movement that gets you away from a screen for a few minutes.

And finally, what about your motivation for the day? This is where you can adopt a simple psychological technique called "implementation intention :" before the day starts (preferably the evening before), you externalize in some way the one or two things you must do the next day. These need to be big, important things. For example, if you have a presentation to do next week, you could decide to make a start on your presentation. Or, if it is the weekend, you may choose to spend all day with your kids.

Whatever you decide must be done the next day, write it down or flag it in your task manager or calendar. If you want to make a significant impact, the thing you decide to do is most likely the thing most on your mind. It could be that you have an issue you need to discuss with a colleague, or you need to call a demanding customer. Make a conscious decision that you will do that tomorrow.

Implementation intention may appear too simple to work; yet it is simple, and it does work. Try it tomorrow. As you read this, decide what two things you will do tomorrow, and write them down. Then, tomorrow morning, remind yourself what those two things are and get on and do them. See what happens.

One of the reasons you may feel demotivated is because you lack a sense of purpose for your day. Using the implementation intention technique changes that. It gives you a purpose, and that changes your perspective.

You don't need to go looking for big, important things to motivate you. All the motivation you need is already inside you. You just need to decide your purpose each day and be open to learning new things.

All of what I have shared with you here is easy. It does involve changing your thinking about your work; it may mean you need to change a few habits, eat fewer carbohydrates, move a little more, and get yourself into bed so you can get enough sleep. It's not impossible. You can change some or all of these things right now if you decide to. It's up to you.

The most important thing is that you begin the day with a clear intention of what you want to get done. That single habit will do incredible things for your overall productivity.

Lessons From Two Prolific Figures

How did Charles Darwin or Winston Churchill get their work done? Both lived in a time before computers and instantaneous communications and yet were prolific in their output. Churchill wrote 37 books, and countless articles and speeches. Charles Darwin wrote one of the most influential scientific books ever written and became the world's foremost expert on barnacles and worms.

How did these people find the time to get their work done? The answer? Both had a structured life that followed a carefully curated daily routine.

Charles Darwin would wake early and go out for a morning walk. He would begin work at 8:00 am and do focused work until lunchtime. After lunch, he would respond to his letters, take his dog for a walk, and take a nap before sitting down to a family dinner. After dinner, he would play card games with his wife before ending his day around 10:30 pm.

Winston Churchill would wake around 7:00 AM and would read the newspapers. Afterwards, he would eat breakfast, dictate letters, or revise a speech. All of this would be done from his bed.

At 11:00 am, he would get up, take a bath, get dressed, and walk before lunch. After lunch, he would work in his home office (study) until 3:30 PM, when he would nap for ninety minutes before having a second bath and getting dressed for dinner.

After dinner, he would return to his study until 1 or 2 AM, when he would retire to bed.

Both men didn't work extraordinarily long hours. Darwin worked around four hours a day, and Churchill around six to seven. Yet both men got a lot of work done.

Part of the reason why they were so productive was because they had a place to do their work. Churchill's bedroom was next door to his study, and Darwin's study was in his home. Working from home in a sanctuary they created was part of the reason they were so productive.

Both Darwin and Churchill compartmentalized their workspace. There was a desk for writing, of course, and in Darwin's case, he had a worktable for studying creatures and plants with his microscope. Churchill had a standing desk for reading proofs of his books and speeches and newspapers – standing desks are not new – and when dictating letters and speeches, he would pace up and down the middle of the room.

However, the key to their prolific productivity was how they limited their access. When working from their homes (Down House in Darwin's case and Chartwell in Churchill's), they ensured the outside world could not contact them except by letter. For us, that would be email today. Letter writing was slow and could be responded to on their terms.

Darwin lived in a pre-telephone world, and while Churchill had access to a telephone, he would not have answered it, and his servants and assistants were instructed not to disturb him. Instead, they took messages and passed them on later.

We feel so overwhelmed and swamped today mostly because we don't limit our access or have a sanctuary from which to produce our work. We allow ourselves to be always available to everyone, so we have little time for deep, focused work. Yet one thing you will notice about all highly productive people today is they not only have a regular place to do their core work but also limit how and when people contact them.

Jeffrey Archer flies to Mallorca, a Spanish island, to write his books on the 27th of December and returns to the UK early in March each year. During those few weeks, he follows a strict structure that involves writing for six to eight hours daily. He writes in the same room that does not have a telephone or computer. During that time you will not find him posting to social media, something he does with impressive regularity the rest of the year.

If you allow yourself to be accessible all day, you will be fighting a losing battle. Your focus will be all over the place, preventing you from concentrating on any one thing.

You may be thinking you have to be available for your boss, customers/clients, or colleagues. But do you? Is there a better way?

When Darwin and Churchill needed to meet with other people, they would head to London for a few days. During those days, they met with the people they needed to talk with and used those days to cram in as many meetings as possible. This was when they were accessible. In Churchill's case, this was weekly; in Darwin's, it was less frequent.

But both ensured that when they did meet with people, it did not interrupt their focused work.

Can you find two or three hours a day where you could cut yourself off from the outside world to get on and do some deep, focused work? Working a typical 8+-hour day would still leave you with five to six hours when you were accessible.

The time management problems we face today are often of our own making. Rather than allowing technology to work for us, we've allowed technology to work *against* us. To get your most meaningful, quality work done, restrict your access. Make it hard to be contacted when you're doing focused work. Limit the channels in which you can be reached – by not being on all instant messaging services – and make sure you have time each day for deep-focused work.

The legendary country singer Dolly Parton can only be contacted by fax! Genius! If you wanted to contact Dolly, you would need to find her fax number AND find a fax machine. That's limiting access on a whole new level.

Charles Darwin and Winston Churchill had a considerable impact on the world and produced enormous amounts of work, yet the total number of hours they worked each day was a lot less than you are likely to work. They did not have access to computers, smartphones, or Google to give them instant access to information. It was a slow, laborious process when they needed to research something.

The only difference between them and you is they restricted their access and built work environments that encouraged deep, focused work. Would your productivity be improved if you adopted just a few of these ideas?

15

Managing Email and Messages

"The price of discipline is always less than the pain of regret." – Robin Sharma

These days, a lot of what you get asked to do will come from email or your company's messaging service. This could be something like Slack, Microsoft Teams, or WhatsApp. How you handle these is important within the whole concept of your system.

One mistake you could make here is to take any actionable message or email and send it to your task manager. The problem with this is you now have a task in two places: it's in your email or messaging app, and it's also in your task manager. When these build up you will find yourself switching back and forth between apps. This is not the most efficient way to manage these.

Before we dig deeper into this, we should first look at the hierarchy of importance with these messages.

It is likely that the more urgent messages you receive will come from your instant messaging service(s). Most people treat these as being more time-sensitive than other types of messages. The exception here is telephone calls, which still remain the medium we are most likely to communicate something genuinely urgent. If your house was on fire, your neighbor would inform you by phone, not instant message.

Next would be messages from services such as Slack or Microsoft Teams. These are similar to instant messages but are less likely to be addressed to you directly. These services are generally used to keep teams informed about what is happening.

And finally, the least urgent method of messaging someone is through email. While there was a time when emailing a person was second only to a phone call in this hierarchy, developments in instant messaging services have relegated email down the list.

If we look at the types of messaging mediums and their order of priority, you will see something like this:

1. Telephone calls.

2. Instant messaging.

3. Slack / Teams.

4. Email.

With telephone calls, you will probably answer them immediately, or at the very least, once you notice you have a missed call. Instant messages could also fall into this category, but for most people, these are likely to be responded to within a reasonably short time.

The types of messages that seem to cause the most difficulty are messages that come through services such as Slack, Microsoft Teams, and Twist. Generally, these are work-related messages and often contain tasks. With these types of tasks, you want to get them into your system as quickly as possible if necessary.

Be careful. Often, these messages just need a response from you. It could be a question to answer or a file to send. With these, you are best leaving them in the messaging service and dealing with them when you have time. Any messages you need time to think about or to find a file or information, you can flag so there is a way to tell you that there is something to do.

> An alternative approach is not to open the message unless you know you will have time to deal with it. When a message comes in, you can see who it is from and the first line or two in the notification window. If you don't have time to do

whatever is asked of you the moment the message comes in, don't open it. This means the little red badge on the messaging app remains on, reminding you that you have unread messages.

All you need do then is have a daily recurring task in your task manager telling you to clear these actionable tasks from your messaging service.

InBox Zero 2.0

What is the best way to manage your emails? Well, I know what *doesn't* work, and that is to have no process at all for managing it. Email is one of those pieces of work that you have little or no control over. You do not know how many emails you will receive today. One thing you can be confident about is it will come, and if you don't do anything with it, it will grow and grow.

Current statistics show the average office worker receives over 80 emails per day, and they are expected to process and deal with those emails quickly and efficiently. Yet, this is not happening. There is so much work that needs to be done; email is checked in the morning, and then the day's business gets underway with meetings, presentation creation, report writing, and more meetings. This means emails pile up in the inbox, making it difficult to distinguish the important from all the rubbish.

Enter *InBox Zero 2.0*. A concept built from the original InBox Zero created by Merlin Mann in 2006. InBox Zero 2.0 adds a little bit more flexibility to the original idea.

The idea behind InBox Zero 2.0, like the original InBox Zero, is your email inbox is sacred territory. No email should ever remain in there once you have looked at it. You only look at an email in your inbox once and immediately decide what it is, what you need to do with it and where it goes. With Inbox Zero 2.0, there are only three places an email can go. Trash, archive, or the Action This Today folder.

Two Simple Questions

Ask yourself: What is it? And what do I need to do with it? Then, do it. Asking these two questions soon becomes instinct and will help you to make a decision in a split second. Once you get faster at asking these questions, you will find processing email takes no time at all.

Trash

This is obvious. If it is not important and it is not of any value to you, then trash it immediately and never give it a second thought. I know this can be difficult at first; you will likely be anxious that you may need it sometime in the future. Fear not; if you received an email, there will be a copy somewhere. In most email applications, anything you delete will remain in your trash folder for thirty days.

Archive

This is where you put emails that need no action from you but may contain some important information you need at a later date. Examples of these could be product information updates, company newsletters or simple updates from your team members.

Action This Day

Your Action This Day folder is for emails you do need to do something with. That could be a reply, or it contains some information you need for the work you are working on, or it could be something you want to read later. If you need to do something with the email, then you put the email in here.

> The phrase "Action This Day" comes from Winston Churchill. During the Second World War, Churchill wrote a lot of memos and letters that were important to the conduct of the war. He also, naturally, received a lot of letters and memos. If there was anything he felt needed immediate attention, he would apply a bright red sticker with the words "ACTION THIS DAY" printed on it in bold, capitalized letters.
>
> As the leader, this was an effective way for Churchill to ensure the right things were being done in the right order.

OPTIONAL: Waiting For

The waiting-for folder is a dangerous folder to have. Why? Because this folder can very quickly become a dumping ground for emails when you are not sure what to do with them. It can also act like a safety net, which ultimately prevents you from developing the skills to make quick decisions about an email.

For some of you, your work may involve sending out requests and waiting for replies. For example, if you work in credit control, sending an email to a client or customer who is a little late in paying their invoice. This is where you would save a copy of the sent email, which would give you a central place to see which ones had been responded to. (Although managing late payers on a spreadsheet would most likely be a better option. Here, you can keep track of who you have written to when and when to expect payment.)

For emails you are waiting for a reply, you can put a copy of the email you sent into your waiting for folder and check this folder periodically. Once the email is replied to, you remove the waiting-for email and place it in the trash or archive. (This should take less than 10 seconds!)

Other Temporary Folders

If you are working on a special, complex project, you may wish to create a temporary folder to hold relevant emails, so it is easier and faster to get to the relevant information. However, once the project is complete, you move the emails into your archive and delete the project folder. These are only temporary folders.

One example of this would be Christmas shopping orders. Place the confirmation emails into a special folder, and once the package arrives, delete the email. This will help you keep track of orders easily. Another use for this folder is travel itineraries. While there are some excellent applications available now that can keep all your important information, having a copy of the original flight and hotel booking confirmations can give you peace of mind.

The key to Inbox Zero is you spend a few minutes a day cleaning up and managing your email, and the rest of the time, you get on with the important work you are employed to do.

However, because handling email and other messages is something you will need to do each day, I've found blocking an hour a day on your calendar for communications will leave you with a lot fewer distractions during the day. Because you know you have an hour later in the day, any email you receive can be placed in your Action this Day folder, and you know you will deal with it during that time.

Letting your email get out of control, with no best practices for managing it, leads to stress as you will always be wondering if there is something important hidden somewhere in there. By keeping a simple, managed system, you will avoid unnecessary stress and will always be able to find what you need.

Search Functionality

Almost all email programs, from Google's Gmail and Apple's Mail to Microsoft's Outlook, have advanced search functions. This means you no longer need to create separate folders for separate types of email. All you need to do is place emails you may want later into your archive, and they will be searchable as and when you need them. It is a good idea to look up the search formulas for the email program you use, as this will help you get so much more out of your email. This is an area that is improving rapidly with the rollout of AI and machine learning.

Email does not need to be a nightmare. It is very easy to get under control. However, as with anything that needs controlling, you do need to put in some processes that help you maintain the system. One such best practice is to get into the habit of always asking

"What is it?" to every email that comes into your inbox, and deciding there and then what you need to do with it. Over time, this becomes automatic, and you will feel uncomfortable leaving an email sitting in your inbox when you know it needs to go into your Action Today folder.

Create a Rule for How Long an Email Remains in your Action This Day Folder

It's all very well moving emails into your Action Today folder, but if you are not doing anything with them, your system will break down. You need to treat any email in your Action Today folder as important and must be dealt with. If you need more than 48 hours to get the necessary information to reply to an email, then send a quick email to the sender so they know you are doing something about it.

If you would like to instantly improve your professional image, this is one of the simplest yet most effective ways to do it. Be consistent, reliable, and prompt with your email replies. The majority of people are so bad at this that the bar is very low. I am surprised how often I get a response from someone with the words "Thank you for your quick reply." It took me 24 hours to reply, and they think that is fast. That's an easy win!

> One of the advantages of starting my working life in hotels was that I was introduced to the importance of consistent standards. I've applied this to my email management process. I have a standard that all actionable emails will be dealt with within 24 hours. If I cannot respond either because I need to get additional information or because I am away, I will always respond to the writer explaining the delay.
>
> To help me with this, I reverse the order of the emails in my Action This Day folder. This means the oldest email is at the top of the list (as opposed to the default, when the newest one is at the top). This means when I open my Action This Day folder, the email I need to respond to next will be at the top and prevents me from cherry-picking the easy ones and leaving the harder, longer responses for later. (A covert form of procrastination!) You can set this up in Outlook and Apple Mail.

If you are not processing your Action Today folder properly, then it will turn into another monster of an Inbox. Don't let that happen. Be strict with yourself.

The Dangerous Two-Minute Rule

There is a "rule" that has been floating around the productivity world for a long time that states: *if you can deal with an email in two minutes or less, then do it now.* There is no point in having these emails hanging around if all it will take is two minutes to reply. Do it and file it.

That sounds logical and does make sense. However, there are a number of problems here. The first is things you anticipate will take two minutes or less rarely do. They frequently take more than two minutes. Secondly, all you need is ten of these emails, and you've spent twenty-plus minutes dealing with them.

When you are processing your inbox, the goal is to clear it as fast as possible. You are processing, not doing. If you keep stopping to respond to what you think is a quick email reply, you are slowing yourself down. With practice, most people can clear fifty to sixty emails in around twenty minutes; that should be the goal. Get your inbox clear so you can get on and do work that matters to you. That means *not* stopping to respond to emails you think will take two minutes or less.

Hard or Soft Email Bankruptcy

There are two ways to get yourself on top of email instantly. The first is to declare a hard email bankruptcy. The second is to declare soft email bankruptcy.

The Hard Email Bankruptcy

This is the scary way. Select all emails older than two weeks and hit the delete key. With the remaining emails, you process them using your new structure (Action This Day, Archive or Delete). Simple, yes? Will you do it? Unlikely, if you are like most people. There is a fear you will delete something important, which prevents you from doing it, although remember, if you have been sent an email, there will be a copy somewhere.

The Soft Email Bankruptcy

The less scary way is to create a new folder called "Old Inbox" and then select all emails older than two weeks and move these to your "old Inbox" folder. These emails will stay in that folder until you do something with them.

Interestingly, most people delete this folder after four or five months because they realize there is nothing important in there after all.

Here is a quick reference guide for managing your emails:

INBOXZERO2

↓

Inbox
All emails come in here first

↓

WHAT IS IT?
Do I need to do anything with it?

No   ## Yes

Archive   Trash

Copy all the emails
currently in your inbox
and paste them in here.
You will go through this
folder as and when you
have time deleting and
filing

Reply

You work from this folder.
This folder contains all
the mails you need to do
something with.

Old Inbox   **Action This Day**   **Forward**

Temporary project folders
Important, current
projects can have their
own temporary folders.

- Read later
- Send to project notes
- Schedule a meeting
- Discuss with a colleague

Waiting For
If you are waiting for a reply,
drag a copy of your sent mail in
here and check this folder
every day

CP
www.carlpullein.com

For most of us, email and messages are a part of our work. Very few occupations give us the luxury of being able to do our work with no form of communication, and very few of us can ignore these messages no matter what position we are in our company. This means depending on how many of these messages come at us each day; we need to allocate an amount of time for dealing with them.

As discussed earlier, if you dedicate around an hour each day to deal with these. And allocate that time to your calendar, you will probably stay on top of your email and messages. For instance, you could set aside 4 pm to 5 pm for communication time. During this hour, you deal with all your messages. That means going through your messages from places like WhatsApp, Slack and Teams, as well as email.

Setting Expectations

The great thing about this approach is that your colleagues, boss, and customers soon learn your routines. It is surprisingly quick how this happens.

The problem you will face if you do not adopt this methodology and instead reply instantaneously is the people you communicate with still learn the pattern of your replies. If you usually reply within the hour to any kind of message and for one reason or another one day you can't, someone, somewhere is going to get upset with you, since you didn't reply when they expected you to.

This is a common misunderstanding I come across in many companies. They think their customers expect a response within a few minutes of sending an email. This is not true unless you have set that expectation, and the problem with setting this kind of expectation is you are not going to be able to respond to your messages within the hour consistently. Firstly, you do not control when you will receive a message, and secondly, you could be driving or in a meeting where you are unable to respond when a message comes in. This kind of commitment is not sustainable.

> In the late 1990s, a company I worked for dismissed the receptionist and installed a new telephone service that enabled anyone to answer the phone when it rang. To ensure the phone was answered, the company set a rule that the phone must be answered within five rings.
>
> In theory, this sounded great – the company saved money by not hiring a receptionist. In practice, it destroyed the company's productivity. Instead of their staff being able to concentrate on their work, every time the phone rang, you could see everyone counting the number of rings. As we

were in a direct customer-facing workplace, it also meant we were unable to give our full and undivided attention to our customers. It was horrendous, and within eight months, the company rehired their receptionist.

By setting times each day for communications, you are managing the expectations of the people you deal with, while putting yourself back in control.

If you work in a job that requires you to respond to messages quickly, one option is to divide your time up in the day. For example, you may want to give yourself thirty minutes before lunch to deal with your morning messages and another thirty minutes before the end of the day to deal with your afternoon messages. This way, no one will be waiting more than two or three hours for a reply. With email, this is easily achievable. With Teams and Slack, I would argue this is within the bounds of reasonableness.

Another way to ensure email and messages do not become a distraction is to communicate with your partners when and how you will respond. A good practice, for instance, is to tell new customers that if something is urgent, they should phone you. Most people are unlikely to phone you, and those who do abuse this invitation can easily be trained by not answering your phone immediately when they do call. Waiting twenty or thirty minutes before responding usually prevents this abuse from continuing. If it does persist, then you may need to have a word with them.

You can change the expectations of your bosses. When I first arrived in Korea, I worked at a language institute that was part of a large chain of institutes in the country. The chairman of the company called me one Saturday morning, and I did not answer the phone. I came from a culture where you did not answer work-related phone calls on a weekend. This had been drilled into me from way back in the early 1990s. There was a clear dividing line between work and personal lives.

The following Monday morning, I called the chairman back around 8 am. His first words to me were in a menacing tone, "I called you, why didn't you answer?" Without thinking, I apologized and explained I didn't look at my phone on a weekend – this was largely true: I was new to the country and had not made any friends at that stage, so there was no reason for me to check my phone. (This was in the days before smartphones. All a mobile phone did in those days was send and receive simple text messages and make phone calls)

However, from that day onwards, the chairman never called me on a weekend.

My naiveté and lack of understanding of Korean culture became an advantage. Even to this day, when a boss or customer calls, you MUST answer immediately in Korean culture. Things are changing slowly, but the sentiment is still there, and I was always surprised when students in my Saturday morning business English class excused themselves whenever they received a call from their boss or customer. They had paid good money to be in that class, yet they allowed themselves to throw that away because they felt obliged to answer their phone while in class.

The strange thing to me was the class was a three-hour class; there was always a break every hour or so. It was unlikely there would be more than an hour before there was a break when they could return a message or a call.

Being *too* available will never serve you. You must and can take control of your time, and this means setting some boundaries – boundaries for when you will be available and when you will not be available.

If you are not setting boundaries, you will not be able to do your most important work consistently. As we looked at in the chapter on time blocking, blocking out time to do focused work allows you time to work on the important work for your day. If you do not truly block time, and that means not answering your calls or responding to your emails and messages while you are doing focused work, you are not going to ever get on top of your work. You will always be behind, and you will always be at the mercy of a random person who doesn't care about what you are doing right now.

The onus is on you to set these boundaries. You need to have the confidence to stand your ground and not respond to every message or email as soon as it comes in. It does not matter where you are in your company's hierarchy. You do have the power to ignore a message, and when you do, and you are consistent with your responses, you will find your boundaries are respected.

I do not usually recommend turning off notifications or removing apps; this always seems a bit extreme to me and takes away the benefit we all gain from the technology in our pockets. But, when you go into a focus session, I would advise turning things off. On some phones, you can turn the screen down, and they won't disturb you; others allow you to turn on a do-not-disturb function where no message alerts will be given for the duration. Use these features.

The great thing about using the do not disturb feature on your phone (and increasingly computers) is when you do finish your focused work session; you can quickly glance at your phone and see what you have missed. You can then decide what needs to be done with those messages. You don't miss anything.

Whenever you fly or are driving, you are unable to respond to messages, and in many instances, you are flying and driving for multiple hours. If you cannot respond in those situations, then you can do it when you are not flying or driving. It's on you to make that choice.

If you do not set a standard now, you are never going to get control of your work and your time. You will remain at the mercy of other people's priorities and that will always disrupt your journey. There is always time for doing your work, and there is time for responding to your messages. You need to decide when you will do those things.

Clear Your Email First Thing

Checking your email first thing in the morning is essential if you are to have a productive day. I know this is contrary to almost all productivity advice. That advice is offered by professors, content creators or productivity experts who have little to no experience working in a world of stressed-out bosses, colleagues, and clients who change important information at the last moment, or anything else vital to your work.

Winston Churchill would have been a wizard at managing email if he had been around today. Churchill always began his day with his mail and the newspapers. Pretty much all the things we are advised not to do. Yet, he wrote 37 books covering seventy-two volumes and thousands of articles in his lifetime. He led the British through their darkest hours during World War Two and still had time to paint and take two-hour lunches and three-hour dinners.

Churchill needed to know what was going on – that was his job. Prepared speeches often needed changing because of some new developments in the world. He would never have been able to make those last-minute changes if he wasn't aware of what was going on in the world before he started doing his planned work for the day.

Email is still the industry standard for communicating between customers, collaborators, and colleagues. It's typically how critical information is sent and how we learn what needs to be done, whether a deadline has changed, or a meeting has been scheduled or cancelled.

The problem with not touching email until later is that you will worry about missing something important. You will constantly think there might be something in your inbox that needs your attention (there probably won't be – rarely does anything need your immediate attention), which will distract you from the work you planned to do.

One of the best times to do focused work is the morning. Your brain is fresh; you are more creative and make better decisions. You destroy this advantage when you are distracted by worrying about what may or may not be sitting in your inbox.

Warning time!

You want to be processing and not doing in the morning. Clearing your inbox and processing it removes the distraction. Processing means deleting, archiving, and moving actionable emails to your Action This Day folder.

Never allow morning email processing to destroy your plan for the day.

And, let me repeat, please forget the 2-minute rule – you only need ten of those, and you've lost twenty minutes – it simply doesn't work for email. The goal is to clear your inbox. To get an idea of what's going on, and then turn to your first task of the day.

The clarity and peace of mind you gain from doing this outweigh the rare possibility you discover an urgent, crisis-ridden email. In the real world, these emails are infrequent, and when you come across one, you can still choose to deal with it later after you have finished your first important piece of work.

The goal here is to clear the decks. Get a grasp on what is happening so you can make any adjustments necessary, so you are working on the right things at the right time. I've seen people panicking to finish a presentation only to discover, after wasting two hours on the presentation file, that there was an email canceling or postponing the presentation until next month.

How much effort and energy does it take to resist the temptation to check your email first thing in the morning? Quite a lot for most people. (That's FOMO – Fear of Missing Out – for you). Instead, you could use a fraction of that energy to resist responding to emails as you process your inbox and, at the same time, get a clear picture of what is happening in your world.

The key to staying on top of these actionable emails is to schedule a period later in the day to respond to them. Give yourself an hour to respond to your communications towards the end of the day. You will avoid email ping pong and be consistent with your responses, so your colleagues, customers, and bosses soon learn your routines, and that makes for a more relaxed working day when you feel much more in control and are less anxious.

16

The Four Levels Of Your Personal Productivity

"Would you tell me, please, which way I ought to go from here?" "That depends a good deal on where you want to get to," said the Cat. "I don't much care where." Said Alice. "Then it doesn't matter which way you go," said the Cat. – Alice's Adventures In Wonderland, by Lewis Carroll

Before we move on, let us look at where you may be in terms of your overall productivity score. It's fun and will give you an idea of where you are and where you want to be.

If you have been reading books and articles, and watching videos on time management and productivity for some time, you will have been developing your skills. However, it is not until you let go of these resources and use the knowledge you have gleaned from them to develop your own way of doing things that you move towards what I term "productivity enlightenment."

Productivity enlightenment is what you are aiming for. This is where you know where everything is; you have a system you developed for yourself, and it works. You are not stressed by the volume of work and requests that come your way, and you have learned how to use the most powerful productivity tool, which is the word "no."

However, before you get there, you are going to pass through three other levels. These are:

Level Zero

The first level is no level at all. It's those people who have no system for managing their tasks or files and only use their calendars to see what meetings have been scheduled for them. These people are unconsciously allowing other people to dictate what they do each day, and they have no interest in building a personal productivity system.

And, of course, Level Zero people will not be reading this book.

The Beginner

Beginners are learning to collect all their tasks into a task manager, and they collect everything. You will find things like *clean the house, check I have my travel card, read a book, reply to Pete's email*, etc. This is great, because the first habit for anyone starting any productivity system is to develop the habit of collecting everything.

It is a learning process. Beginners need to develop the proper habits and techniques, so it is good that everything is collected at this stage. Beginners usually do a weekly planning session, but it is sporadic and often skipped. Processing their inbox is done fastidiously, and there's a lot of experimentation with tags/labels and project folders.

It is important that the beginner does this, and testing and trying the many ways you can improve your time management and productivity will ultimately help you settle on a system that works for you.

The Intermediate

Intermediates are people who are now testing every new productivity app on the market. With each new app they try, they will probably spend a whole day transferring their tasks from the previous app to the new app and then the rest of the week tweaking and playing around with the new features they have.

This is also a good practice. Testing out these new apps, while doing nothing for their productivity, teaches them what features they find useful and which elements don't work for them.

The intermediates will join forums or Facebook groups to find interesting new ideas to try out. While this will do nothing to help them get their work done, it does help them see what works and what does not work for them.

Rather interestingly, the intermediate stops doing a weekly planning session – they don't yet see its value. The only times they will do any planning session (or weekly review) is when either their system breaks down – which always happens when no weekly planning session is done – or when they switch apps.

Graduating from this level can take as long as three to four years, and that's when things become interesting.

At this stage, people divide into two groups. The first group ends up micro-managing everything in their task managers or calendars. Everything is meticulously collected into a system – most of which will be repeatedly rescheduled, and the rest dumped into a project folder, never to see the light of day again. These people find themselves overwhelmed and frequently falling off the productivity wagon.

Again, this is primarily a learning process. People soon discover that dumping everything into their task manager doesn't work, and they eventually find themselves at the next level.

However, there is danger lurking in level three. This is because, sometimes, a person never progresses to the next level. They become trapped testing and trying new apps, never being able to make up their minds about what works and what does not work. Part of going through this level is to find the kind of app that works for *you*; if you are always attracted to the latest new app or system, you will never progress to the next level. At some point, you need to make a decision.

The way out of this level is to understand that apps are only containers for your system. What matters is how you manage your tasks, events, and notes. No app is going to do that for you. You have to do that. You decide where something goes, and you should not be relying on an app's so-called artificial intelligence or machine learning to do that for you.

The Enlightened Ones

The enlightened ones finally discover that personal productivity is about eliminating the unimportant and only focusing on work that aligns with their areas of focus and achieves their goals. Being at the enlightened level means you know what is important. You know what you are striving for, and you are clear about the path you are going on. You are clear about which tasks are meaningful and which ones can be dropped and deleted, and you have no fear of doing that.

You can tell who these people are because they have a small number of tasks on their task list each day – usually, around four to five tasks. They allow nobody except themselves to control what goes on their calendars, and they block a significant amount of time off for deep, focused work each day, including weekends.

The enlightened ones never miss their weekly planning sessions. It's a core part of their week, and you will find they complete these sessions either early Saturday or Sunday morning. They understand that to remain focused on their vital work and achieve their goals, they must make sure they are progressing towards them each week, and the only way to do that is to do their weekly planning sessions consistently.

The most obvious sign you are in the presence of an enlightened one is they are incredibly relaxed and calm. Nothing seems to bother them. They are decisive, write everything down, are seldom if ever late for anything, and have learned how to politely say no to additional commitments.

To reach this level of productivity requires knowing what is important to you, to understand what you want out of life, and to know why it is important to you. Without knowing that, you will become entangled in other people's projects, goals, and crises, and you will find your task manager is full of other people's tasks with very few of your own.

> *[Leadership is] learning what you can control and what you cannot, and not wasting time on what you cannot control.*
> – Christian Horner, Red Bull Formula 1 Team Principle

You can test this. How many of your tasks in your task manager benefit someone else? Look for tasks related to writing reports for your boss and responding to client or colleague emails. Now, compare that to the number of tasks that directly drive your goals and core work forward. If you are doing more tasks for other people and not enough tasks that directly contribute to *your* goals and core work, you need to realign your priorities.

The enlightened ones are focused on their purpose, goals, and areas of focus first, and everything else comes a distant second. It's these places where you will find satisfaction, fulfilment, and an unbelievable sense of calm.

The most productive people have not changed any of their productivity tools for years. They understand that the tools are meaningless when it comes to performing at your very best every day. David Allen, who has used the same task manager for twenty years, can you imagine how fast he is using his tools after twenty years of use? Jack Dorsey, the former Twitter CEO, has been using Apple Notes for all his productivity needs for at least ten years. Simple, and it works beautifully for him.

You can, of course, shortcut this process considerably if you understand that the purpose of becoming better at time management as well as more productive is never about being able to do more work in less time; that's a fool's goal and one you will never achieve. It's about eliminating as many less important and unnecessary tasks and only allowing meaningful, goal-accomplishing tasks onto your task list.

It takes time to learn this, and it helps if you know what is important, and what your areas of focus are. Once you know what these are, you can make the necessary adjustments and start enhancing your life, achieving your goals, and being a lot less overwhelmed.

You do not need elaborate tools to become enlightened. You do need to know what is essential and have a determination to eliminate anything that does not contribute towards your higher purpose. You do not need the latest, shiniest application to achieve that. This is why many of the most productive people don't need a task manager at all. They have a notebook, or they use the built-in notes apps on their phone and their calendar. It is because they know exactly what they want and have a plan on how to achieve it.

Your progress through these levels takes time, and it's important to let that time pass. Keep working on developing your system. Refine it and make it faster and more efficient. Once you have learned the basic steps (collect, organize, and do), focus your efforts and energy on making these steps instinctive.

When you start the day, you start knowing what needs to be done. When you end the day, you end it with a plan for tomorrow, and you maximize your time doing what needs doing.

And remember, it's not all about work. One of the wonderful things about being at the enlightened level is that you have more time for rest and relaxation! You recognize when you need to rest and take it easy, and you take that rest. Because you are organized and you know where you are with all your commitments, you take that rest without feeling guilty or anxious. And believe me, it's a wonderful feeling!

17

The Real "Secret" To Getting Things Done

"The battalion's operating premise was that the best way to take care of soldiers was to build standards and processes into a routine until predictable things worked smoothly." – General Stanley McChrystal

Throughout this book, I have given you a complete productivity system and explained how you can avoid the common pitfalls many people face. You now have everything you need to build your own system, a system that works for *you*. There are a few additional tips that may help you.

Many productivity systems promise to help you get your work done. New apps appear daily, promising they will make you more productive, and countless blog posts, YouTube videos and podcasts tell you to try this or that new innovative idea.

The truth is, *the only way you will get more done is to do more*. No new app, system, or idea will ever replace that simple fact.

But there is a problem with this, in a way, counter to the culture we live in today. We are supposed to take more breaks, be gentler with ourselves to protect our mental health, and slow down when we feel tired. All good advice, but it does not help us to be more productive if to be more productive means we have to do more.

So, what can you do to do more in a gentler, human-friendly way?

The secret lies in *building processes*. There are a number of tasks we regularly perform for our work. That could be contacting prospects if you are a salesperson, performing medical exams if you are a doctor, or preparing a lesson plan if you are a teacher. No matter what you are employed to do, there will be a set of core tasks you are expected to perform.

It is these core tasks you want to turn into automatic processes.

Part of the reason you will struggle to get more done is the time thinking about what to do. Without a plan for the day, it's surprising how much time is wasted thinking about what to work on. This usually leads to working on the least important task because it's easy and can be done in a few minutes. So, the thinking goes, if I just get this little task done, it will get me started. But it doesn't, does it? Once that little ten-minute task is done, you then waste another five to ten minutes looking to see what to do next, and that is repeated multiple times per day.

If you want to get more done, reduce the time trying to decide what to work on. The way to do that is to *have a plan and a process for your day.* Having fixed times each week for doing the work that matters will ensure you get the work done and removes a lot of stress. When you know you have time to do the work you must do, you stop worrying about it. You just get on and do it.

The "secret" to getting more done is reducing the number of decisions you need to make. In other words, deciding in advance what gets done, so you do not have to make as many decisions during the day.

You do need to keep things flexible. Things never go according to plan. Emergencies will happen, unknown urgent tasks will pop up every day, and things will go wrong.

And if there are no emergencies? You've just given yourself some spare time. You can either have a nap, go for a walk, or dip into your task manager and pick something you want to do.

The advantage of building a process for your day is that you will find better ways of doing the work as time goes by. The consistency you now have will free your mind to develop better, more effective strategies for doing the work

Imagine part of your core work is to write a blog post for your company's website each week. For this you may block an hour each Monday for writing the draft. Then, on Tuesday, you block another hour for editing and posting. Now, you've given yourself a process and protected time for getting it done. Do that every week, and you will soon find yourself getting faster at producing a weekly blog post.

That's what having a process does: it gives you time to get better and faster at doing your work. When you can do your work better and faster, you free up time to do more (or not if you wish). Now *that's* the secret to getting more done!

Now, How To Do *Less*

Traditional to-do lists don't work. You know this, right? They don't work because most of the tasks on to-do lists are mundane, low-value tasks that move very little forward.

The key to better task management is in being strategic about what goes on your task list. Clearly written and thought-out high-value tasks that move you towards the outcomes you want should be dominating, not low-value tasks that are moved to a project folder, never to see the light of day again.

The biggest failure with traditional to-do lists, though, is they soon become too long and overwhelming, and then you stop looking at them, which means they are no longer useful.

So, what can you do to make your task list more effective and shorter?

Make Use of Checklists

A lot of the work we do is routine. For instance, I create YouTube videos each week. There is a process for creating a YouTube video, from the planning to the recording and editing. I could put each step into my task manager, but when I am recording a video, all I need to know is its time to record the video.

Part of recording the video is to check the settings on my camera, the lighting, and the sound. I could put all those checks in my task manager, too, but they would be worthless there. All I need is a checklist in my notes app to make sure I am doing the right things in the correct order and a date on my calendar for a two-hour block to do the recording. I combine that checklist with the plan for the video, and this ensures I consistently complete my recording without missing any steps.

Checklists do not need to be in your task manager. You can hold checklists such as a packing list, a morning routine list or a closing down routine in your notes app or journal. These can be copied for each new session, and you can add any relevant notes to the list. Again, all you need in your task manager is a single task telling you to begin a particular process.

Use Your Calendar

Your calendar should contain all your fixed, time-specific work and appointments. Things like appointments naturally go on your calendar, but you should also use your calendar for timed blocks of work and for dealing with your communications and daily admin.

Doing this means you not only have the required time for doing your important work, but it also means you do not need to have tasks in your task manager telling you to do this important work.

The rule is: what goes on your calendar gets done, and once something is on your calendar, you know you have time for doing it. You can relax.

Use Your Notes App

Managing all your project tasks inside a to-do list is asking for trouble. Tasks will be added, moved to a project folder, and then get lost in the shuffle. To avoid this, you are likely to add a random date, so at least you will be reminded of a task you think needs doing on a date in the future – only to reschedule the task once it comes back up to another random date.

Instead of all this organizing and reorganizing, just create a project note in your notes app. In this note, you can keep all your relevant information on the project, add links to files you are working on, and notes about what needs to happen next.

In your task manager, have a single task telling you to work on or review a particular project. Then you open up your project note, and you will quickly see what needs to happen next, and you can get straight to work.

If you have to contact someone about a project, you can add that task to your task manager with a clear description. For example, "contact Nicola about the slide design for next week's presentation." This way, the task is a unique task with a clear outcome, which makes it a lot more motivating to do.

Of all your productivity tools, your task manager is the one that needs to be the cleanest and tightest. Only have tasks that you know you need to do and make sure they are clearly written and any dates you have added to them are real dates, and not just random dates you have picked out of the air, so you do not forget to do them.

When you begin the day with a task list that is clear, relevant, and achievable, you will have a lot less on there, it will be more focused, and you are much more likely to clear your day's list.

There are a lot of tips and suggestions in this book, and if you follow these, you will quickly find you have more available time and get more of your important work done. However, don't try and change everything all at once. That is a recipe for failure. Instead, pick one area and develop that. Begin by transferring all your project notes and tasks into your notes app. If you have been maintaining all your project tasks in your task manager, this will be the most difficult habit to change. It will be uncomfortable at first but stick with it. You can then replace all those project tasks in your task manager with a single task telling you to work on or review a given project and link your project note to the task.

> Most task managers will allow you to create clickable links. I've found the best way to link project notes to tasks is to connect the note to your task as a clickable link.

> Notes apps such as Evernote, Notion, Apple Notes and OneNote all allow you to get a unique URL link to the note and you can then paste that into your task.

Another first step is to promote your calendar to the CEO position of your productivity system. This is the one tool that will always tell you the truth about how much time you have. Trust it, let it do its job and never ignore it. Digital calendars can send you notifications fifteen or thirty minutes before an event to remind you to begin doing a type of activity or that you have an appointment. Use these tools. They take a lot of stress out of your day and release you from a lot of stuff you are holding on to in your head.

When you start with these small changes and give yourself sufficient time to allow them to become habitual, you can then move on to modifying and evolving your system.

From now on, I strongly recommend you make a commitment to give yourself thirty to forty minutes every Saturday morning to plan for the following week. Review your calendar, look at your active projects, and ensure you have sufficient time to complete your core work. Things will change throughout the week – there will always be unexpected emergencies, but the plan you put in place is there to ensure you know where you are and what needs to be done, and ultimately, that the right things are getting done each week. You won't complete everything you planned to do; that's fine. The important thing is you got most of what you wanted to do done.

And finally, enjoy the process of taking control of your time! Be strong, and do not let other people hijack your time. It's your life, and it's your time. Nobody can take that away, so be intentional, say "no" more than you say "yes" (a great habit to develop), and always remember your life is so much more than just your work.

I will leave you with this brilliant quote from Computer Science Professor Randy Pausch two months before he passed away from cancer.

> *"It is not the things we do in life that we regret on our deathbed. It is the things we do not. I assure you I've done a lot of really stupid things, and none of them bother me. All the mistakes, and all the dopey things, and all the times I was embarrassed – they don't matter. What matters is that I can kind of look back and say: Pretty much any time I got the chance to do something cool I tried to grab for it – and that's where my solace comes from."*

INDEX

220

CREDITS

Philip Jan Rothstein, FBCI, is President of **Rothstein Associates Inc.**, a management consultancy he founded in 1984 as a pioneer in the disciplines of Business Continuity and Disaster Recovery. He is also the Executive Publisher of **Rothstein Publishing**.

Editorial Advisory Services

Kristen Noakes-Fry

Indexing

Enid Zafran, Indexing Partners LLC

Cover Design and Graphics

RangKyoung Im

Sheila Kwiatek, Flower Grafix

eBook Design & Production

Donna Luther, Metadata Prime

ROTHSTEIN PUBLISHING
A Division of Rothstein Associates Inc.

ABOUT ROTHSTEIN PUBLISHING

ROTHSTEIN PUBLISHING is the premier global content provider since 1989 in the core disciplines of Business Continuity Management; Emergency Management; Disaster Recovery and Prevention; Information Security; Risk Management; Crisis Communications, Crisis Management and Crisis Leadership.

More recently we've established ourselves as a serious publisher in the fields of Productivity; Time Management; Cybersecurity; Critical Infrastructure; Business Strategy; and Leadership.

Our founder **Philip Jan Rothstein, FBCI**, is an internationally known management consultant, entrepreneur, columnist, and publisher of or contributor to 100+ books.

Our authors are globally recognized; several are uniquely distinguished international thought leaders as founders of their respective industries. Most have also been key participants in developing industry standards and best practices. Some are founding fellows of the Business Continuity Institute, as is our publisher, Philip Jan Rothstein, who was elected a Fellow in 1994 in recognition of his substantial contributions to the profession.

Rothstein Publishing is a division **of Rothstein Associates Inc.**, an international management consultancy founded in 1984.

ROTHSTEIN
PUBLISHING
A Division of Rothstein Associates Inc.

ABOUT THE AUTHOR

Carl Pullein is not just another time management "expert;" he is the visionary behind the groundbreaking **Time Sector System™** and the **COD™** task management system, meticulously crafted for the demands of the 21st century.

He was voted the **world's #1 time management professional for 2024** by www.GlobalGurus.org.

What Carl Does

With a global reach, Carl helps organizations and individuals worldwide master time management and boost productivity.

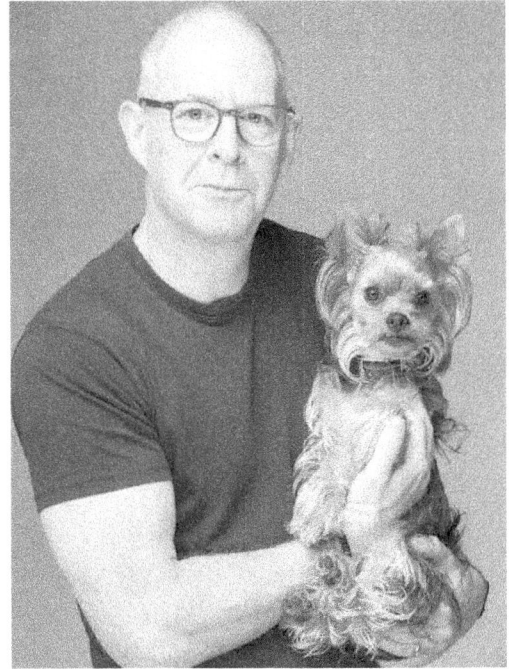

Carl's Mission

Carl is committed to equipping people with the tools needed to take control of their time and concentrate on their priorities. His content, including YouTube videos, presentations, and immersive workshops, offers a unique blend of interactivity, entertainment, and education.

Carl is passionate about nurturing and guiding individuals on their journeys; he is incredibly fortunate to have embarked on this fulfilling career in none other than South Korea – an electrifying and captivating country that brims with exceptional talent and is home to some of the world's most prestigious companies.

His academic journey began with a Bachelor's Honours Degree in Law from Leeds Metropolitan University in the UK, which gave him a solid foundation to pursue various roles. Beyond academia, he proudly serves as an advisor to the Sunfull Movement, an organization dedicated to stamping out online bullying, a cause that resonates deeply with him.

His passion for mentorship extends to the airwaves as well. You'll occasionally find him lending his coaching insights and help on the 1013 Main Street Radio show for TBS eFM in Korea, where he helps guide university students on the path to securing their dream jobs. It's a privilege for Carl to be part of their journey toward success.

When he's not immersed in the world of mentorship, training, and coaching, you can catch him cheering on the Leeds Rhinos Rugby League team.

Carl enjoys motor racing, especially Formula 1 and the World Rally Championship (WRC). He also likes hitting the pavement as a dedicated runner, participating in marathons not only across Korea but also in far-flung corners of the globe.

His love for adventure extends to the great outdoors as well, exploring the Korean mountains with his wife and his faithful canine companion, Louis. He also enjoys Trance music, and the many exhilarating EDM festivals in Korea.

Ready to transform your relationship with time? Discover Carl's transformative resources and coaching services by visiting his website today. Your journey to greater productivity awaits!

www.carlpullein.com

www.ingramcontent.com/pod-product-compliance
Lightning Source LLC
Chambersburg PA
CBHW061230150426

42812CB00054BA/2554